FOO   S'

NAPA VALLEY

Help Us Keep This Guide Up to Date

We would love to hear from you concerning your experiences with this guide and how you feel it could be improved and kept up to date. Please send your comments and suggestions to:

editorial@GlobePequot.com

Thanks for your input, and happy travels!

FOOD LOVERS' SERIES

FOOD LOVERS'
GUIDE TO
NAPA VALLEY

The Best Restaurants, Markets & Local Culinary Offerings

1st Edition

Jean Saylor Doppenberg

gpp

Guilford, Connecticut

Copyright © 2012 Morris Book Publishing, LLC

Editor: Amy Lyons
Project Editor: Lynn Zelem
Layout Artist: Mary Ballachino
Text Design: Sheryl Kober
Illustrations © Jill Butler with additional art by Carleen Moira Powell and MaryAnn Dubé
Map: Daniel Lloyd © Morris Book Publishing, LLC

ISBN 978-0-7627-7315-2

Printed in the United States of America
10 9 8 7 6 5 4 3 2 1

All the information in this guidebook is subject to change. We recommend that you call ahead to obtain current information before traveling.

Contents

Recipes, 217

Apricot Tart with Cornmeal Crust (Knickerbockers' Oak Avenue Catering), 239

Meyer Lemon & Ancho Chile Chicken (Chef Hannah Bauman of Round Pond Estate), 242

About the Author

Jean Saylor Doppenberg has been eating her way through California's Wine Country in general—and Napa Valley in particular—for more than two decades. Though the legendary 9-course, sit-down dinner at the French Laundry still eludes her, she has nonetheless logged several thousand miles exploring the renowned Valley to partake of its burgers, burritos, biscotti, and brownies. She is the author of *Insiders' Guide to California's Wine Country* (Globe Pequot Press), and has also written about food for the *Napa Valley Register*. Jean lives in Sonoma County, Napa's neighbor.

Acknowledgments

Keeping track of whom to thank for helping me write this first edition was not an easy task. I've interviewed so many people along the way. Many stand out, however, for their insider knowledge and years of experience running wineries, cheffing, baking, farming, conducting business, and living in Napa Valley.

The following friendly people were gracious with their time and patience, even while I was asking the nitpicky questions: Mary Jo Geitner, Marie Bianco, Tyffani Peters, Annie Baker, Julie Ann Kodmur, Sally and Jeff Manfredi, Kim Daniels, Patti McBride, Colette Hatch, Spencer Reid, Summer Sebastiani, Steve Sando, Ken and Susie Pope, Joanne Blicker, Eric G. Hensel, Lana Richardson, Carrie Baker, Craig DiFonzo, Michael Cope, Chris Aken, David Zurowski, Sandy Dominguez, Dominic Orsini, Ethan Bier, Gillian and Nick Kite, Laddie Hall, Sommer Woolley, Bob Hattich, Lynn Brown, Barbara Clerici, Mark Haberger, Maria Haug, Brad Gates, Lizzie Moore, Sherri Hurley, Cathy Hammond, Diane Padoven, Beth Ponder, Katrina Kirkham, Sally Wood, Sandra Barros, Melissa Welles, Sean Knight, and Bertram Whitman.

Thanks also to my husband, Loren, and my sister, Jan Blanchard, who shared in some of my exhaustive fact-gathering and food-devouring trips up and down the Valley—all in the name of research. I also appreciate the many friends who weighed in with their opinions and advice, and provided the cheerleading and the laughter necessary to keep me going: Jan, Mariann, Donna, Julia, Pat, Cathy, Kathy K., Lynn, Kathy M., Linda, Karen, Doris, Sandy, Phyllis, Michele, Ed, Riki, Nancy, Connie, Sue, and Monica. And to Mom and Dad, thanks for all those great home-cooked meals.

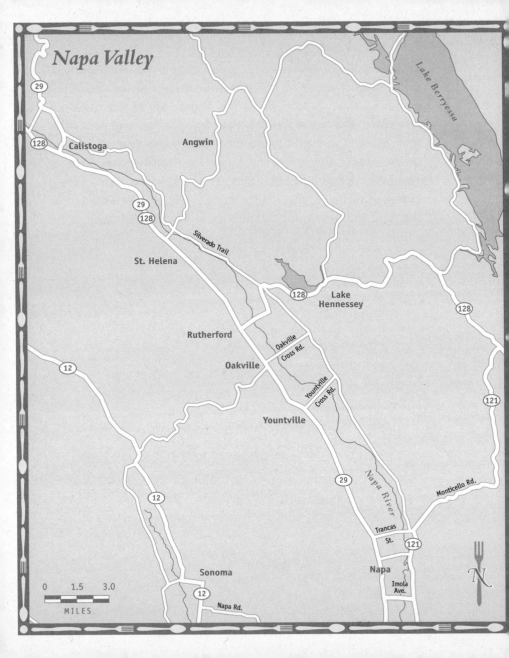

Introduction

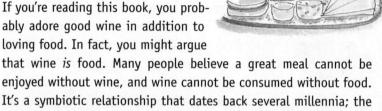

If you're reading this book, you probably adore good wine in addition to
loving food. In fact, you might argue
that wine *is* food. Many people believe a great meal cannot be
enjoyed without wine, and wine cannot be consumed without food.
It's a symbiotic relationship that dates back several millennia; the
first archaeological evidence of wine production is from 8,000 years
ago in Eurasia.

In Napa Valley, winemaking has been going on for consider-
ably less time—not yet 200 years. An early settler, George Yount
(Yountville is named after him), first began to grow grapes in the
mid-1800s. Nearly all of the wine grapes George and his peers produced at that time were crushed into simple jug wines.

Fast-forward a century, to the 1960s. Business mavericks such as
Robert Mondavi led the charge for attracting visitors to Napa Valley
by the thousands and marketing the region like crazy. A fearless
and tireless self-promoter, Mondavi built a sleek, California mission-
style winery in Oakville and gave away free tastes of his product
(alas, tasting is no longer free). Following quickly in his footsteps
were scores of visionaries who designed and erected wineries to
match—or surpass—those found in France, Italy, and Germany.
More showplace wineries have opened for business in the last 25

years. Consequently, much of what you see as you drive through Napa Valley is relatively new.

For more than 50 years, the wine grape has been the engine driving the economy of Napa Valley. Before that, orchards of fig and walnut trees were plentiful, along with fields of wheat, and wine grapes made up only about a third of the crops grown. As the decades ticked away, orchards were cut down in favor of vineyards, and the price of farmland crept ever upward, making it economically impractical to grow anything but profitable wine grapes. In 2000, a golf course along the Silverado Trail was even plowed under to make way for more Cabernet Sauvignon grapes—Napa Valley's star varietal. The frenzy to plant vineyards reached a crescendo in the early 2000s, and premium wine grapes now account for 98 percent of the agriculture in the Valley.

Twenty years ago, even as visitors were coming by the millions to view the vineyards and pack the tasting rooms, world-class dining experiences were few and far between. But now there are so many great options, it's difficult to choose between them. High-profile chefs such as Thomas Keller, Cindy Pawlcyn, Ken Frank, Michael Chiarello, Richard Reddington, Christopher Kostow—and more recently Tyler Florence and Masaharu Morimoto—have helped Napa Valley evolve into one of America's leading culinary destinations.

How to Use This Book

Organized into five chapters, this guide begins with the city of Napa at the south end of Napa Valley. This first chapter also includes a few attractions south of the city, as well as the restaurants, farms, and food-and-wine pairing opportunities found in the Carneros wine-growing district southwest of Napa.

Back on the main drag, Highway 29, the focus is on the towns you'll pass through as you drive north from the city of Napa. That includes chapters on Yountville, the Oakville/Rutherford region, the town of St. Helena, and Calistoga. Each chapter features some or most of the following categories:

Landmark Eateries

These are the restaurants you've heard about, read about, and perhaps hope to dine at someday, several started by famous chefs you might recognize from their popularity on television and the attention they receive online. Others are established eateries with longtime, loyal followings. One small Napa Valley town has had more Michelin stars per capita awarded to its restaurants (six in 2011) than anywhere else on the planet. These are significant culinary experiences, if it's within your budget.

Foodie Faves

Offering delicious meals as varied as deli sandwiches, ahi tuna burgers, and Thai specialties, these eateries are easier on the wallet than the Landmark Eateries, and just as filling. Some may still have white linen tablecloths and a sommelier on staff, but the haute cuisine factor is dialed down somewhat. This category also includes the mobile vendors who dish out delectable food from vintage Airstream trailers and other customized vehicles.

Restaurant Price Key

So you have some idea how to budget for your meal, Landmark Eateries and Foodie Faves follow this pricing guide:

$	inexpensive; most entrees under $15
$$	moderate; most entrees $15 to $25
$$$	expensive; most entrees $25 to $35
$$$$	very expensive; most entrees more than $35, and prix-fixe menus of $50 or more per person (not including wine pairings)

Specialty Stores & Markets

Seeking artisanal cheese and bread, olive oil tastings, stores with exceptional wine collections, fresh-roasted organic coffee, or the pots and pans necessary to prepare your own world-class cuisine? If it's all of the above, Napa Valley doesn't disappoint. This category includes grocers with a gourmet spin, stores selling every type of kitchen utensil imaginable, the diverse and popular Oxbow Public Market in Napa, coffee roasters, bakeries, ice cream merchants, and other food purveyors.

Farmers' Markets & Farm Stands

Napa Valley's agricultural focus is predominately wine grapes, but the seasonal farmers' markets in Napa, St. Helena, and Calistoga are great places to pick up heirloom vegetables, flowers, and locally produced sweet and savory foods. Several produce stands can also be found around the Valley at ranches and farms. Most of the family farms request that you call ahead before dropping by, and many will give tours and explain their methods of growing fruits and vegetables and raising animals. In addition to having websites, several of the farmers maintain Facebook pages to keep customers abreast of what's going on and to take orders for fresh eggs or produce.

Made or Grown Here

Napa Valley has become an incubator for food-focused cottage industries, with entrepreneurial innovators crafting artisanal products. Their jams, jellies, chocolates, cookies, and other goodies are available in stores around the Valley and also online.

Food & Wine Pairings/Landmark Wineries

It's not practical, nor possible, to write a book about Napa Valley food without including Napa Valley wines. The two go together like strawberries and cream. Fortunately, many wineries offer food-and-wine pairings to enhance their tours and tastings. Advance reservations are usually required, as these popular attractions tend to fill up rapidly with visitors thirsty for wine education and craving small bites of well-matched food. This category also features weekly or monthly events that usually don't require prior reservations—just show up and join in the fun. Several historic, showplace, and quaint family-run wineries, open regular hours or by appointment, are also included here. (Take note: "By appointment only" sounds more forbidding than it really is. The type of permit held by a winery dictates whether it can operate a tasting room that is open to the public for walk-in visitors, or by appointment only. For the latter, a quick call to the winery from the side of the road—perhaps even at the entrance to the property—might suffice.)

Brewpubs & Microbreweries
A lot of wine is poured in Napa Valley—a lot of wine—but beer lovers haven't been forgotten. And it's no secret that winemakers usually crave beer when they're off duty. There's a much-quoted expression in Napa Valley: It takes a lot of good beer to make great wine. Try these locally brewed suds served alongside great meals, if desired.

Learn to Cook

One of the premier schools for chefs, the Culinary Institute of America, has an outpost in St. Helena that offers classes for the professional chef de cuisine or the casual home cook. Other options are available throughout the Valley, ranging from intimate hands-on groups to classroom-style instruction. Either way, you can count on a good time while learning to prepare a scrumptious meal. For the city of Napa, this category includes special walking tours, too.

Getting Around

If you develop a case of the munchies in Napa Valley, you're never too far from a restaurant, cafe, bakery, gourmet grocer, farmers' market, or other food purveyor that can satisfy your cravings. Moving between these many choices in the Valley's small towns is best achieved by car, as most of the action is found along or slightly off one main road, Highway 29, which spans a distance of approximately 30 miles from south to north through Napa Valley.

The highway is four-lane, quasi-freeway-style in the southern part of Napa County and around the city of Napa. It then narrows to two lanes a few miles ahead at Yountville. This forces drivers to slow down and enjoy the scenery of this rural region.

The views are awe-inspiring, but on Saturday and Sunday the congestion on Highway 29 north of Yountville can try your patience, particularly on holiday weekends. The alternate route to the east is the Silverado Trail, which is two lanes wide and parallel to Highway 29 the entire distance between the city of Napa and the town of Calistoga. Both roads have occasional dips and tight turns, and the savvy driver is always on the lookout for bicyclists along some of the narrow shoulders. Napa Valley is a popular training site for both professional and amateur cyclists, so please be mindful of the two-wheelers sharing the road with you.

So slow down and enjoy the ride. It may take more time than you first assume to drive directly from, say, the Oxbow Public Market in Napa to the Craftsman Inn in Calistoga, but there will be irresistible opportunities to pull over and check out other attractions along the way. Parking is abundant almost everywhere you go, and nearly always free.

To avoid confusion, be aware that Highway 29 is also referred to as "St. Helena Highway," generally north of Yountville, and that's reflected in several physical addresses in this book. The expression "Upvalley" is also common parlance among locals, usually in the city of Napa, and you may hear it often in your travels here. It refers to the area of the Napa Valley north of Yountville.

Keeping Up with Food News

Free printed information about Napa Valley's food scene and its other attractions can be found in winery tasting rooms, visitors' centers, stores, and other places where tourists tend to gather. Online review sites and blogs are also helpful resources, particularly if the participants remain objective and don't abuse their anonymity and merely rant. Bear in mind that comments by diners on sites such as Yelp.com can yo-yo from five stars to one star within hours of each other, leaving you wondering if a restaurant is worth trying or not. Even on the same night in the same trattoria, some diners might have a great experience and others may be disappointed. It's inevitable.

The added bonus of online information is its immediacy. Many restaurants, wineries, stores, farmers, mobile food vendors, and other food purveyors also use Facebook and Twitter to keep their fans and customers updated about events, sales, and other news.

The list below is a starting point, representing some of the publications and blogs that keep their information about Napa Valley reasonably fresh and unbiased.

www.BiteClubEats.com: As an online branch of the *Santa Rosa Press Democrat,* Sonoma County's largest newspaper, this site primarily covers that county's food scene. But because Sonoma County residents often cross the county line to dine, the latest Napa Valley restaurant news—high-profile changes in chefs and cuisine, and recent closings and openings—is usually mentioned on this blog.

The Cork Board, http://uncork29.com/blog: Maintained by a group of Napa Valley residents, this site is updated frequently with useful tips. It includes "Cork Bits"—suggestions for weekend events at wineries.

http://InsideScoopsf.sfgate.com: An offshoot of the *San Francisco Chronicle,* Inside Scoop concentrates primarily on the restaurant goings-on in the city of San Francisco. But the newspaper's restaurant critic also blogs about the latest changes in Napa Valley's culinary scene.

Napa Valley Guidebook, in print and online at www.legendary napavalley.com: You might spot this one free around the Valley, particularly if you step into the Napa Valley Welcome Center (at 600 Main St. in downtown Napa). Published annually as the official guide of the Napa Valley Destination Council, the magazine is oversized, glossy, and full of lovely photographs, lists, and even some fold-out maps. It's also downloadable from the website.

Napa Valley Life, in print and online at http://napavalley lifemagazine.com: This glossy, full-color magazine is features-oriented, with articles about food and wine, green living, interior design, art, and personal fitness and health—most of it taking place in the Valley. Published six times a year, the magazine also includes a helpful community calendar and a few winery maps and lush photographs of Napa Valley.

http://NapaValleyRegister.com/inv: The Napa-based daily news-paper, the *Napa Valley Register,* produces a quarterly insert called "Inside Napa Valley." The information is aimed at both locals and visitors, with features on food, wine, art, cooking, and lists of win-eries and coming events. If you can't find the print version where other free tourist information is on display, the magazine is acces-sible from the newspaper's website.

The Preiser Key to Napa Valley, in print and online at http:// preiserkey.com: The Preiser family compiles this magazine, distrib-uting 250,000 copies every year (three issues annually) in about 500 locations in Napa and Sonoma counties and in San Francisco, too. Printed on sturdy, non-glossy stock in full color, the *Preiser Key* is data-heavy and impressively comprehensive. The long lists of wineries and restaurants are attractively arranged alongside informative articles on wine statistics and wine appreciation, brief reviews of restaurants and wineries, and detailed maps.

Wine Country This Week, in print and online at www.wine countrythisweek.com: With winery maps, articles about wineries, a list of wineries, and a calendar of events, this magazine jams a lot of information into 80-some weekly pages, and it's been published since 1981. It also covers a lot of territory, literally. Besides Napa Valley, the magazine has information on wineries and attractions in Sonoma County and the wine-growing areas of Mendocino and Lake Counties, neighboring Suisun Valley and Yolo County wine regions, the Livermore-Lodi-Woodbridge area, and even the Sierra Foothills wine scene.

Food Events & Happenings

Festivals and celebrations that spotlight wine in Napa Valley usually come with a tasty bonus: generous food pairings or full-blown, sit-down lunches or dinners. In this section I list a few where you can count on great nibbles to be served. Many are annual events; some are more exclusive to visitors or locals who make advance reservations to take part in once-in-a-lifetime opportunities.

March

A Taste of Yountville, along Washington Street in Yountville, CA 94599; (707) 944-0904; www.yountville.com. Some of the bigger food-and-wine fests in the region get more attention, but this event on a Saturday is one of the most satisfying. Move from one site to another (there are five event sites with booths) to sample interesting bites from the dozen or so restaurants in town and sips of wine poured by more than 20 nearby wineries. There's no admission fee, but tasting tickets for food and wine are $1 each. A garden tour of the French Laundry's 2 acres of culinary herbs and produce is also available. A ribs-and-links barbecue is sponsored by the fire department, too, and live bands provide entertainment throughout the day. Cleanse your culture palate by taking a walk through the community center to view works by dozens of Yountville and Napa Valley artists. The event runs from 11 a.m. to 5 p.m.

April

April in Carneros, (800) 909-4352; www.carneroswineries.org.
Over one weekend in mid-April, approximately 20 wineries in
the Carneros grape-growing district, or appellation as we call it
around here, celebrate with open houses. Some of the participating
wineries are rarely open to visitors except at this event. The fun
includes food-and-wine pairings, live music, art shows, discounts
on wine, and other special attractions. The nibbles might range
from fig sausages to sliders to plate after plate of artisanal cheeses.
The $35-per-person tickets (purchased in advance) are nearly all-
inclusive (a few wineries may charge additional fees for special
activities or extra offerings). Proceeds from the event help to fund
scholarships at Napa Valley College and Santa Rosa Junior College.
Note: A majority of the participating wineries are over the Napa
County line into Sonoma County—the two counties share the
Carneros appellation.

Discover Wine Day at Robert Mondavi Winery, 7801 St.
Helena Hwy. (Hwy. 29), Oakville, CA 94562; (888) 766-6328; www
.robertmondavi.com/discover. Discover Wine Day began as a tribute
to Mondavi, who left quite a legacy in Napa Valley when he died in
2008. On a Saturday in spring, visitors can tour the winery free of
charge and receive a complimentary glass of wine, too. Other events
during the day (from 10 a.m. to 5 p.m.) cost from $15 to $50 per
person. These might include seminars on food-and-wine pairings,
chef's demonstrations, wine cellar tastings, and perhaps a cookbook
signing (in 2011, wine expert and Food Network personality Ted
Allen was a featured guest). Count on live music, too.

Forni Brown Welsh Gardens Annual Spring Sale, 1214 Pine St. (at Cedar St.), Calistoga, CA 94515; (707) 942-6123. As I watch a smiling Lynn Brown gently toss granulated fish emulsion onto hundreds of potted vegetable starts, I realize he loves his work and really knows what he's doing. He should—as one of the owners, Lynn has been cultivating vegetables like this for more than 30 years and dispensing expert advice, too. (Visitor: "My yard is shady by late afternoon and can get chilly on summer nights, so what's the best tomato variety for me to try?" Lynn, without hesitation: "The Russian Black, definitely.") On several weekends in April and May, the greenhouses at this small, regionally famous farming business are bursting with starter plants for home gardeners. Row after row of 4-inch pots hold scores of varieties of heirloom tomatoes, peppers, herbs, squash, pumpkins, and many other vegetables—all at bargain prices and ready for planting. Seeds, larger containers of plants, and organic fertilizer are also sold. **Forni Brown Welsh Gardens** (see the listing in Made or Grown Here in the Calistoga chapter) is not a nursery, per se. They grow the salad greens and other produce served in some of the best restaurants in Napa Valley and the San Francisco Bay Area, and so are not usually open to the public. The owners hatched the idea of an annual sale because diners in their clients' restaurants were asking where they could find the same delicious greens to use in their own cooking. Down through the years the popularity of the sale has grown mostly by word of mouth, and it attracts gardeners from throughout the region who are seeking the best vegetable starts around.

Kitchens in the Vineyards Annual Home Tour, (707) 258-5559; www.musicinthevineyards.org. Though the lineup of open kitchens changes from year to year, the cause is always the same: to raise money for the Music in the Vineyards' Chamber Music Festival held in August. Spend about 6 hours on a Saturday touring five fabulous homes with some of the jazziest kitchens around, along with dining rooms, entertainment areas, and gardens, too. While gawking at the kitchens of your dreams, you'll be nibbling on small bites provided by top Napa Valley chefs and also meeting cookbook authors available to sign their books. Tickets for the tour are $65 per person. The night before the tour, a preview party is held to visit the homes, followed by a wine reception and dinner ($165 per person). Reservations are required for both events.

Rutherford Grange Crab Feed, Rutherford Grange Hall, 8550 St. Helena Hwy. (Hwy. 29), Rutherford, CA 94573; (707) 265-9180. Rural grange halls such as this one along the highway in Rutherford are disappearing in many communities, the victims of old age and neglect. But Rutherford is renovating its Grange and raising as much money as it can to give the building a new lease on life while maintaining its historical charm. The Grange serves the area year-round as an inexpensive rental for weddings and special events, and it's a polling station on election days. Believed to be about a hundred years old, the building has required substantial repairs and upgrades, and the stucco façade that was added in the 1960s is being peeled off to reveal near-pristine redwood shingles underneath. So an annual crab feed was launched to help pay for the $200,000-plus rebirth. Raising money for this good cause is both tasty and soul-satisfying. Tickets are $35 for adults and $10 for children 15 and under. For that amount you receive a generous helping of freshly cooked crab, salad, garlic bread, and pasta. Drink tickets are extra. A happy hour precedes the dinner, which starts at approximately 3:30 p.m. An auction and prizes are also part of the fund-raising fun.

May

Annual Fair Housing Napa Valley Pasta Sauce Cook-Off, 601 Cabot Way, Napa, CA 94559; (707) 224-9720; www.napa-fairhousing.org. All nonprofit organizations struggle these days to raise funds to operate and serve their communities. Fair Housing Napa Valley is no exception. With the proceeds collected at this annual event, which takes place on a Saturday night in mid-May, FHNV can continue to work toward eliminating housing discrimination and ensure equal housing opportunities for everyone in Napa Valley. This is one event where amateur chefs get to shine and are encouraged to enter their homemade pasta sauce for judging by the attendees. The winning chef receives a magnum of, perhaps, Diamond Creek Cabernet Sauvignon; the second-place prize might

be two bottles of Judd's Hill wine. The $35-per-person fee includes dinner, wine, and live music. Covenant Presbyterian Church on Salvador Avenue is the venue.

Appellation St. Helena's Annual Ultimate Blind Date Wine Tasting, Charles Krug Winery, 2800 Main St. (Hwy. 29), St. Helena, CA 94574; (707) 963-6045; www.appellationsthelena .com. Save this one Saturday afternoon, from 2 to 5 p.m., to taste more than 60 limited-production wines made from grapes in the St. Helena AVA, or appellation. Meet the winemakers, too. The event's name is a play on words: it's a blind tasting and so touted as a "blind date—wine country style." The blind tasting is optional, but if you choose to participate in guessing the varietal, vintage, and producer of brown-bagged bottles, you become eligible for the grand prize: $2,000 worth of St. Helena–appellation wines for your cellar. In 2011, Cindy Pawlcyn was the chef behind the event's food, with goodies from her three Napa Valley restaurants: Cindy's Backstreet Kitchen, Go Fish, and Mustards Grill (Go Fish has reopened by Cindy as Brassica Mediterranean Kitchen and Wine Bar). Proceeds are donated to a local nonprofit organization that offers assistance and work placement to vineyard and migrant workers. Tickets are $60 per person, purchased in advance online.

Cheers! St. Helena, www.cheerssthelena.com. On the first Friday of the month for half the year (the warmest half, May through October), from 6 to 8 p.m., downtown St. Helena becomes a party zone. As many as five stages come alive with music, and three short streets off Main Street are closed to traffic. It's free to walk around, but wine tasting is $35 per person for many generous sips. Restaurants supply some sidewalk food, and shops get in on the wine-pouring fun. It's a great way to meet people, try munchies from the town's famous eateries, and soak up the atmosphere of the town.

Rutherford Appellation Wineries Spring Passport Weekend, www.rutherford-appellation-wineries.com, or www.rutherforddust.org. From 11 a.m. to 4 p.m. on a spring Saturday and Sunday, participants nosh on brunch-type cuisine to go along with multiple tastes of wine at 16 or so hosting wineries, some not usually open for public tastings. Proceeds are donated to worthy Napa Valley charities such as Napa Crime Stoppers, the Rutherford River Restoration Project, and the Rutherford Volunteer Fire Department. To keep the event from becoming overcrowded, a limited number of "passports" are sold. Ticket holders receive their instructions for the weekend when they purchase online. A similar event is held in December; check the website for details.

Tamale Festival, Cedar Street and Pioneer Park, Calistoga, CA 94515; (707) 942-6206; www.calistogafamilycenter.org. Coinciding with Cinco de Mayo, the one-day Tamale Festival on a Sunday is a benefit for the Calistoga Family Center. Tamales are a popular celebratory dish in Mexico and Central America, created in layers and consisting of a ground-corn dough spread on a corn husk or banana leaf and then steamed. As many as 10 to 12 local chefs might have several different kinds of savory tamales to sample (chicken, pork, beef, cheese and chili, and vegetable) and maybe some fruit-filled tamales for variety. Classes in expert tamale creation are conducted, along with amateur and professional contests for the best tamales. There's live music and activities for the kids, too, including vigorous piñata bashing. It's free to attend, then pay as you go for the tamales and other food and beverages. The fun starts at 11 a.m., wrapping up at 4 p.m.

June

Auction Napa Valley, Meadowood, 900 Meadowood Ln., St. Helena, CA 94574; (707) 963-3388; www.napavintners.com. In 2011, this auction passed the $100-million milestone—the amount of money it has raised during the past 31 years for local health-care agencies and other good causes within Napa Valley. It's always been considered the premier wine auction event in the nation, though another, younger wine auction in Florida has lately been surpassing this one's annual take by a few million dollars. Auction Napa Valley is a series of events during the first weekend in June, Thursday through Sunday. This usually includes exclusive dinners on Thursday with winemakers. A barrel auction, held at the Culinary Institute of America on Friday, sets this wine auction apart from others. The barrel auction's haul alone in 2011 was $1.2 million, adding significantly to the overall auction's $7.3 million total. Meadowood resort is where the big and boisterous live auction takes place on Saturday, with scores of "lots" up for grabs to the bidders with the deepest pockets. The combination of goodies in the lots can be alluring as the frenzied bidding is moved along by animated auctioneers and the occasional celebrity cheerleader (Jay Leno and Dana Carvey in past years). In addition to some cool cult wines and diamond earrings, one lot might also include a trip to Maui *and* a winter ski vacation in Utah, both via private jet, of course. That particular lot was purchased for $140,000. Despite the high cost to participate in the auction weekend ($2,500 per person for all of the events), tickets are in great demand and sell out quickly. Less expensive tickets are available for fewer events. The Napa Valley

Vintners association runs the show each year, and their website is the place to go for information.

July

Home Winemakers Classic, Charles Krug Winery, 2800 Main St. (Hwy. 29), St. Helena, CA 94574; (707) 738-7132; www.drycreek .org. One of the longest-running annual events in Napa Valley (30 years in 2012) is a salute to amateur winemakers. From 4 to 6:30 p.m. on a Saturday, a local winery is the setting (in 2011, it was Charles Krug). This "poor man's wine auction" is an affordable way to taste great wines from home winemakers throughout California and watch the judging of more than 100 wines by local vintners and other wine professionals. There's also food and music, a raffle, and a silent auction. Advance tickets are $35 (or $45 at the door). The proceeds benefit the all-volunteer Dry Creek-Lokoya Fire Department, whose territory is 200 square miles of steep and rugged terrain in the western hills of Napa County.

Napa County Fair, 1435 N. Oak St., Calistoga, CA 94515; (707) 942-5111; www.napacountyfairgrounds.com. This is Napa County's only county fair, at its official county fairgrounds (not to be confused with the Town & Country Fair that takes place annually in the city of Napa). Scheduled around the weekend nearest the Fourth of July, the fair runs three full days (after opening night). Food isn't the main event, but there is plenty of wine tasting. The rest of the attractions are what you expect in a good homegrown fair: arts-and-crafts exhibits, carnival rides, farm animals on display, sprint car racing, live music, and booming fireworks.

Napa Valley Art & Music Festival, Trinchero Family Estates, 100 St. Helena Hwy. (Hwy. 29), St. Helena, CA 94574; www.nvamf .org. The inaugural event took place in 2011, a fundraiser for the St. Helena Rotary. Art in all forms is on display, created by 100 artists from around the nation and local talent, too. Paintings, sculptures, ceramics, photography, fiber arts, and many other media are judged for a top prize of $1,000. Bring the whole family—there's an activity area for children, too. Several rock bands perform over the 2-day event, open from 10 a.m. to 6 p.m. each day. Pay for the food, beer, and wine as you go. A night-before gala ($100 per person) kicks off the weekend.

August

Napa Town & Country Fair, Napa Valley Expo, 575 Third Street, Napa, CA 94559; (707) 253-4900; www.napavalleyexpo.com. "Homespun Fun" was the theme of the 2011 fair, so that gives you some idea of the type of shindig this is. Though not the official Napa County fair (that takes place in Calistoga), standard fair activities can be expected, from livestock judging to a carnival, as well as name entertainment (Big Bad Voodoo Daddy and country star Marty Stuart have taken the stage). Scheduled over 5 days— Wednesday through Sunday—in mid-August, admission is $13 for adults, $10 for youngsters and seniors, and free for kids 5 and under. Food lovers might want to come hungry to the Preview Gala and Wine Tasting that takes place the night before the fair kicks off. For $25, you receive a souvenir wineglass and move from table to table, enjoying pours of wine and the culinary creations of many chefs and caterers. The gala is a fundraising event for the Friends of the Fair Foundation.

Blues, Brews & BBQ Festival, www.donapa.com. Bring along your dancing shoes and prepare to get down with some of the San Francisco Bay Area's best blues musicians on three different stages along First Street on a Saturday afternoon in late August. The beer is supplied by 20 or more microbreweries, some of them small-production brands. The barbecued food is plentiful, from turkey legs to tri-tip. Grab a cold one and a good spot to cheer on a local celebrity in the rib-eating contest.

Cochon Heritage Fire, Charles Krug Winery, 2800 Main St. (Hwy. 29), St. Helena, CA 94574; www.cochon555.com. Carnivores, start your grills. On a summer Saturday afternoon, Cochon Heritage Fire celebrates the art of butchering, fire cooking, and consuming whole animals and all their nasty bits at a local winery (Charles Krug in 2011). If you don't mind the sight of dismembered hog heads, the sound of hacksaws ripping through bone, and the overwhelming aroma of cooked bacon, this event is made for you (*cochon* is French for pig). It's a culinary competition and tasting event that's mostly about sustaining heritage pig diversity and encouraging participants to think about where their meat comes from and the importance of supporting local food producers. There's plenty of pork, but many other meaty smells fill the air. As many as 25 chefs and 10 butchers from around Napa Valley and the nation will turn the spits, roasting nearly a ton of meat over wood fires—heritage beef, goat, lamb, chickens, rabbits, and more. The beer and wine flow freely, but the main focus is on meat. Heritage Fire is one of several similar competitions held around the nation during the year organized by Cochon 555 (visit the website for more information). Open to the public, tickets are $100 per person to sample cooked meats, wines, craft beers, and watch butcher demonstrations (VIP tickets, at $200 per person, include extra goodies and earlier admission to the event).

September

Annual Napa River Wine & Crafts Fair, www.donapa.com. This fair on a Saturday in mid-September is one of the oldest in Napa Valley, celebrating its 35th year in 2011, and also the largest one-day event you'll see in Napa. The arts and crafts are the attraction, of course, and as many as 25,000 people also attend to enjoy the live music and wine tasting. Expect about 140 arts-and-crafts booths, along with food vendors serving primarily pre-packaged food. Third Street downtown is the center of the action.

Annual Napa Valley Aloha Festival, www.manaleohcf.org. Can't make it to Hawaii? The Manaleo Hawaiian Cultural Foundation of Napa brings Hawaii to you, at the Napa Expo, 575 First Street, on a Saturday in mid-September. The family-oriented event spotlights Hawaiian and Polynesian culture with authentic foods, music and dance, arts, crafts, and activities such as lei making. Proceeds from the event are used to fund scholarships in education. The festival also supports the local food bank, so donations of nonperishable food are encouraged. Admission is free, and so is the parking.

Tastings on the Lawn, Charles Krug Winery, 2800 Main St. (Hwy. 29), St. Helena, CA 94574; (707) 967-2229; www.charleskrug.com. The beautiful grounds of this winery are turned into a big food- and wine-tasting party for 3 hours on a Saturday afternoon in September. The winery has been throwing this annual shindig for 60 years, and it is much anticipated by locals and visitors. About 15 of the winery's current releases are available for tasting along with generous food pairings. Because the 2011 event was also a bit of a celebration for the winery's 150th birthday, it was a given that the personal cellar of president and CEO Peter Mondavi Sr. would be raided to share some of his well-aged treasures with the attendees. A live band provides the entertainment, and dancing is encouraged. Bring along your lawn chairs, hats, and blankets for getting comfortable and staying awhile. Tickets are $30 per person in advance, $35 at the door.

October

Downtown Blues Weekend, various venues in Calistoga, CA 94515; (866) 306-5588; www.calistogavisitors.com. The 3 days of music and food commence on a Thursday evening, with restaurants hosting winemaker dinners. That's when the chef, along with a vineyard representative, talk about the meal you are about to eat and how it pairs with that particular winery's product. On Friday it's Calistoga Night Out, with live blues bands performing around the town and the downtown shops staying open late to serve appetizers. Saturday's full afternoon of live blues takes place on an outdoor stage, coupled with wine tasting. The outdoor music is free; wine tasting runs about $30 per person for a generous number of tastes, along with a souvenir glass. Sunday's events are primarily brunches at the town's restaurants, with even more live blues performances.

November

Flavor! Napa Valley Celebration of Wine, Food & Fun, Culinary Institute of America at Greystone (CIA), 2555 Main St. (Hwy. 29), St. Helena, CA 94574; www.flavornapavalley.com. The inaugural Flavor! took place in autumn 2011, featuring numerous epicurean and oenophile events at the CIA location and at Silverado Resort and Spa in Napa. Many of Napa Valley's celebrity chefs take part in this 4-day celebration of food and wine, including Thomas Keller, Michael Chiarello, Ken Frank, Cindy Pawlcyn, Tyler Florence, Masaharu Morimoto, and Christopher Kostow. Many of these world-class food artists are also CIA graduates, and proceeds from this event benefits the CIA's financial aid for students. The Silverado Resort and Spa is the major founding sponsor. Tickets range from $95 to $1,000 for each demonstration, wine tasting, or dinner event.

City of Napa

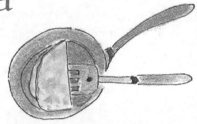

Ten years ago, visitors to Napa Valley used to drive right on past Highway 29's exits to the city of Napa, stepping on the gas to quickly reach the more desirable small towns Upvalley with better restaurants, niftier spa resorts, and jazzier shopping opportunities.

The change in Napa city in a single decade has been remarkable: new gourmet restaurants with celebrity chefs, a lively food and wine center (the Oxbow Public Market), more upscale lodgings, and even the promise of a Ritz-Carlton hotel still to be built downtown on Silverado Trail. A Ritz-Carlton, in the city of Napa? The locals would have laughed at that proposal once, but now it seems like a good fit.

As the largest city in Napa Valley (population 76,915), Napa is also where most of the county's commerce and government is based. But when it was founded in 1836, there wasn't much to brag about. In fact, Napa floundered until a certain precious metal was discovered in 1848 in California's Sierra mountain foothills, and the Gold Rush was on. Some directionally challenged gold-seekers got lost after leaving San Francisco on their way to the mines. Instead of heading east 100 miles, they mistakenly meandered north roughly 40 miles and landed in Napa. Many remained to eke out a living, and the town's population began to climb.

The city of Napa's early prosperity can be attributed to the river that runs through it. Before the days of bridges and roads, freight and visitors both came and went by boat between San Francisco and Napa, and Sacramento and Napa (via the Sacramento River). In the mid-1800s Napa Valley farmers were cultivating fruits and vegetables and acres and acres of wheat. These were all valuable commodities to the San Francisco markets, particularly the wheat. Even ships from foreign ports came for the wheat. Wine grapes were still a minor crop.

In fact, Napa's early history was more beer-driven than wine-driven. Two big breweries in the town were pumping out huge quantities of beer, because hops and barley were being harvested in abundance in the Valley. When the Gold Rush brought fortune hunters by the thousands to San Francisco, hops and barley were in greater demand to make even more beer for the thirsty travelers. The Napa River was the route for getting these beer-making grains to San Francisco. Napa's waterfront was a busy place, with agricultural products stacked high awaiting shipment to growing cities and towns in northern California.

With the crops bringing in the bucks and visitors coming for the fresh air and the scenery, industry increased along the Napa River with tanneries, iron works, and potteries, among

others. The men who controlled the money, the bankers, erected extravagant homes to show off their wealth. Many of the commercial buildings and mansions from that era still exist, refreshed with 20th-century makeovers and reopened as chic inns, shops, and restaurants.

In the late 1990s, winery baron Robert Mondavi contributed a huge sum of money to build a food, wine, and art center in downtown Napa along the Napa River. When it finally opened in 2001, Copia, as it was called, helped to jumpstart new development and renovation in the lackluster core of the city. Copia's upscale restaurant, Julia's Kitchen (named for and inspired by beloved chef Julia Child), opened to great fanfare, and there were a few other restaurants in the city generating acclaim. At about the same time, a massive flood control project along the Napa River got under way, which would eventually reshape parts of the riverbank, relocate several businesses, and lead to new commercial buildings.

Yet the food scene in the city of Napa even a few years ago left many visitors unsatisfied. With the exceptions of a popular steakhouse at the county airport, a French restaurant on the edge of downtown, and Julia's Kitchen (all now closed), desirable dining was limited. Many entrepreneurs and chefs recognized Napa's potential, however, and one by one, new plans for high-end eateries, shops, and hotels were put into motion.

Unable to attract the thousands of tourists and locals it needed to survive, Copia was forced into bankruptcy in 2008 (Julia's

Kitchen was also a casualty), and it now sits empty and silent next to the newer and immensely popular Oxbow Public Market. Rumors fly every few months about the Copia building's future: the Food Network wants to buy it, or the Culinary Institute of America is interested in using it as another West Coast campus. Copia's 3.5 acres of culinary gardens have not been abandoned, fortunately, and several local chefs are harvesting the perennial herbs and citrus and nut-bearing trees originally planted there—and adding a few crops of their own—while the holders of the deed decide how to move forward in a sluggish real estate market.

Though there have been some speed bumps along the way, the city of Napa is now its own destination. Instead of driving by, many travelers to Napa Valley are exiting the highway into Napa and finding plenty of reasons to stay.

Landmark Eateries

Bistro Don Giovanni, 4110 Howard Ln. (at Hwy. 29), Napa, CA 94558; (707) 224-3300; www.bistrodongiovanni.com; $$$. Just north of Napa along Highway 29, Bistro Don Giovanni is one of those popular restaurants that people loved from the beginning (since 1993), and they keep coming back for more. The place is roomy, with seating for 160. There are fireplaces inside and out, along with a covered patio. The grounds overlook vineyards, and include a large garden with herbs and vegetables used in the kitchen. The conversation-starting Commedia dell'arte fountain is the centerpiece outside, with the characters of a traditional 16th-century Italian improvisational theater swinging from poles and playfully splashing around. Proprietor Donna Scala was born into a hotel and restaurant family, and she studied cooking in the south of France. Along with husband Giovanni, she operated a restaurant in Yountville in the late 1980s before opening this favorite of locals. On the menu are such choices as *rigatoni con polpette* and *bucatini carbonara*, four types of pizza, beet and green-bean salad, antipasti and carpaccio, and fish options, too. The Scalas emphasize service, believing it is a huge part of a fine dining experience. Open daily for lunch and dinner.

Celadon, 500 Main St., Napa, CA 94559; (707) 254-9690; www .celadonnapa.com; $$$. Lovely, lush plantings make the patio area really delightful on a warm day. Located in the Napa Mill complex along the Napa River, Celadon's cuisine has influences of the Mediterranean, Asia, and the Americas. Small plates might include flash-fried calamari with spicy chipotle chile glaze and pickled ginger, or macadamia nut–crusted goat cheese with port-poached figs, apples, and crostini. Moving up to big plates, make your choice from beef, duck, sole, chicken, and pork selections. The restaurant is also known for its specialty cocktails, such as the prickly pear margarita and the blackberry sidecar. Celadon is led by Greg Cole, who also owns and operates **Cole's Chop House** (see next listing). He began his career working with chef Phillippe Jeanty at Domaine Chandon in Yountville. Open for lunch and dinner daily.

Cole's Chop House, 1122 Main St., Napa, CA 94559; (707) 224-6328; www.coleschophouse.com; $$$. Red meat, and plenty of it—that's why chef and owner Greg Cole calls his namesake restaurant a "classic American steakhouse," and it's elegant, too. The building dates from the 1880s, made from native stone and with the original open-truss ceiling and Douglas fir floors. Dining is available on two levels, as well as on a seasonal patio. There's also an impressive mahogany bar where martinis and cocktails are expertly shaken and stirred. Order the oysters Rockefeller, reputed to be some of the best ever tasted in these parts, while waiting for your table. The largest steaks, for big appetites, are 21- or 28-day dry-aged slabs of rib eye, New York cut, and porterhouse. A bone-in rib eye, New Zealand lamb chops, and center-cut pork chop are equally delicious. Alternatives to the red meat are salmon and a seafood-of-the-day choice—even a short stack of rosemary-scented portobello mushroom caps. Sides of creamed spinach or thin-sliced onion rings pair well with the steaks, and the baked potatoes are huge. For a sweet ending, ask for bananas Foster. If you really enjoy the experience at Cole's, Greg will sell you some nifty logo merchandise, including a set of steak knives. Open for dinner daily.

Farm, 4048 Carneros/Sonoma Hwy. (Hwy. 12/121), Napa, CA 94559; (707) 299-4880; www.thecarnerosinn.com; $$$. Generally considered to be a romantic spot—and attached to the high-end Carneros Inn resort—Farm is refined in a spacious, barnlike structure. One wall is dominated by a huge fireplace, and outside is a fire pit for before- or after-dinner reflection. The place has been called glitzy, high tech, and country all under one roof. On the menu are regional oysters, Rocky Jr. chicken from neighboring Sonoma County, duck breast, prime filet with bone marrow, Maine lobster, and Scottish salmon. Fresh lamb can be expected here in spring, too. For dessert, save room for the mascarpone and espresso parfait with shaved dark chocolate. The resort's less-expensive **Boon Fly Cafe** is nearby (see Foodie Faves). Along the highway, watch for the red building that comes into view rather quickly as you zip along—that's the entrance to the resort and restaurant. Open Wed through Sun for dinner.

La Toque, 1314 McKinstry St., Napa, CA 94559; (707) 257-5157; www.latoque.com; $$$. Once located farther north in Napa Valley, La Toque moved to the city of Napa when the new Westin Verasa hotel opened adjacent to the Oxbow Public Market. If you're hesitant to dine in a hotel restaurant, don't be. La Toque was legendary before it relocated in 2008, and its reputation is still stellar. Chef Ken Frank earned a one-star rating in the 2011 *Michelin Guide* for the San Francisco Bay Area, so you can count on a great meal. In spring, a typical menu might include chilled asparagus with sauce gribiche; pan-roasted duck breast with cherry, chocolate nib, and red-wine sauce; Yukon Gold potatoes; and sautéed strawberry crepes. Instead of ordering a single entree, create your own chef's menu, selecting three or four of the savory dishes, plus dessert, for a fixed price. That way you can sample different "mains" when you can't decide on just one. Most of the ingredients on the menu are sourced locally, from nearby farmers and other food purveyors in northern California. Chef Frank has a way with truffles, too, offering annual truffle menus: in fall, white truffles get star billing, and black truffles take over in January. Open for dinner every night.

Morimoto Napa, 610 Main St., Napa, CA 94559; (707) 252-1600; www.morimotonapa.com; $$$$. You'd think that Napans and regular visitors would have "celebrity chef fatigue," what with all the big culinary names helming new restaurants in the Valley in the past few years. Yet this predominately seafood restaurant created by a major food television star, Iron Chef Masaharu Morimoto, has been dazzling diners since its large double doors opened in 2010, with no drop in popularity noticed yet. The draw? Sushi, for sure, but many other specialties such as sea urchin carbonara, rock shrimp tempura, and toro tartare are also hot menu items. Some of the fish is flown in from Tokyo three or four times a week. Chef Morimoto believes in adding European and Western cooking techniques to traditional Japanese fare, so many dishes are a fusion of flavors (such as *foie gras* Takoyaki—Japanese dumplings made with *foie gras* instead of octopus). The chef operates six other restaurants around the world, all with different menus. Dinner is served every night, typically to midnight or later; lunch is available Wed through Sun.

Rotisserie and Wine, 720 Main St., Napa, CA 94559; (707) 254-8500; www.rotisserieandwine.com; $$$. Behind the Tyler Florence retail shop in the Riverfront complex is the chef's newest restaurant, with big windows and a patio facing the Napa River. Butcher-style drawings of beef cattle loom on the walls, and the chandeliers made from wine barrels, also found in his store next door, light up the dining room. Starters include beef tartare and chicken-fried chicken liver. The meats mostly come off a rotisserie, including chicken, lamb ribs, porchetta, and prime rib. The meat board changes daily, but it might feature sweetbread terrine or headcheese and oxtail in gelée. Among several side dishes are the bone marrow gratinée with caramelized shallot and green apple, and slow-cooked collards. The duck confit waffle is served with egg, cracklings, and bourbon cask–aged maple. If not automatically delivered to your table when you are first seated, ask for the corn sticks. The servers are dressed casually, much as you might be, in jeans and plaid shirts. Open for dinner every night.

Ubuntu, 1140 Main St., Napa, CA 94559; (707) 251-5656; www .ubuntunapa.com; $$. When Ubuntu opened a few years ago, it was a curiosity—a vegetarian eatery and a yoga studio, with some avant-garde sculptures sprinkled around. The praise came fast and from on high: *New York Times* food critic Frank Bruni placed Ubuntu at number 2 on the newspaper's list of "Most Intriguing New Restaurants Outside New York City." Vegetarian cuisine is elevated to an art form at Ubuntu, which sources most of its produce from biodynamic gardens nearby and other ingredients from local purveyors, such as Rancho Gordo New World Specialty Food (chef Aaron London makes a stew from their Yellow Eye heirloom beans, infusing it with many vegetables and seasonings). Other choices on the menu could be slow-roasted beets and broccoli, pasta with artichokes and caramelized grapefruit, and artichoke vichyssoise. Chef London also smokes blue cheese in-house with applewood chips to use as a base for his roasted beet and avocado salad. Open for dinner nightly, and weekends for lunch and dinner.

Foodie Faves

Andie's Cafe, 1042 Freeway Dr., Napa, CA 94558; (707) 259-1107; www.andiescafe.com; $. Just off Highway 29 at the First Street exit is this small eatery with a big menu. The hamburgers, tacos, corn dogs, chicken fingers, burritos, and breakfast sandwiches are popular with the locals (who hope this place won't be "discovered"). Near the Napa Outlet mall, Andie's is next door to a car wash, so you can get your wheels scrubbed while you enjoy a Marin or Monterey burger. Open daily for breakfast, lunch, and dinner.

Angèle, 540 Main St., Napa, CA 94559; (707) 252-8115; www .angelerestaurant.com; $$$. Angèle is located in what used to be a boathouse about a century ago. The patio is awesome, right along the Napa River, and big, too—with seating for 65. The food is French, but with special spins applied by Chef Patrick Kelly. Open the meal with *foie gras au torchon* with caramelized pineapple and  candied pistachios, or the pasta bolognese with braised rabbit, pork belly, and wild mushrooms. Main courses are mouthwatering: Sonoma duck breast, *boeuf bourguignon,* roasted rabbit, and pancetta-wrapped guinea hen. Celebrating 9 years in business in 2011, Angèle is generally credited with jumpstarting the no-end-in-sight gourmet restaurant boom in downtown Napa, an area once nearly deserted at the dinner hour. Open daily for lunch and dinner.

Avia Kitchen in the Avia Hotel, 1450 First St., Napa, CA 94559; (707) 224-3900; www.aviahotels.com; $$. Hotel restaurants sometimes get a bum rap, regarded as a last resort for a meal. Avia Kitchen isn't like that. In fact, in the hands of Executive Chef Chris Aken, this restaurant does not disappoint. Open for breakfast and dinner daily, the setting and the decor are delightful, including the coziness of a fireplace and patio dining. Breakfast options range from traditional eggs, potatoes, and toast to brioche French toast and Belgian waffles. Choices on the dinner menu include portobello fries with black-truffle aioli; seared lamb loin with eggplant, tomatoes, and artichokes; beef ragout with potato gnocchi and mushrooms; and risotto with morel mushrooms. A charcuterie plate is available, as well as a *fromage* selection and an antipasto platter. Much of the produce featured in the dishes is grown in Napa, so it's exceptionally fresh. The hotel's wine bar, called the Riddling Rack, starts serving goodies at 3 p.m., including a few of the same items on the dinner menu, along with organic popcorn in three flavors—great for satisfying the before-dinner munchies. There's even special plush seating for chess players, if the spirit moves you. See Chef Chris Aken's recipe for **Seared Scallops with Warm Crab Beurre Blanc** on p. 229.

Azzurro Pizzeria, 1260 Main St., Napa, CA 94559; (707) 255-5552; www.azzurropizzeria.com; $. One word: *manciata,* folded and eaten like a sandwich. It's a handful of just-baked dough with a salad on top—a classic Caesar, a spinach salad, arugula with blue cheese, or Italian style with salami and provolone drizzled with oregano vinaigrette. The pizza menu sticks with popular choices, such as the *rosso, margherita, verde, bianco,* Sicilian, *funghi, pollo,* and *primavera.* There's pasta, too, including orecchiette ("little ears"), with spinach, garlic, and chiles. The owners and chefs all spent their earlier years training in kitchens overseen by big-name San Francisco and

Napa Valley chefs such as Bradley Ogden and Cindy Pawlcyn. Open for lunch and dinner every day.

BarBersQ, 3900-D Bel Aire Plaza, Napa, CA 94558; (707) 224-6600; www.barbersq.com; $$. Napa Valley isn't known as a hot spot for barbecue joints, so your options are limited. But in the case of BarBersQ, you can't go wrong. Select from Memphis-style pulled-pork sandwiches, briskets, ribs, and all the fixins, such as collard greens, cornbread, and macaroni and cheese. Begin the meal with chicken wings or gumbo, or salads such as Caesar, Cobb, or the wedge—iceberg lettuce with blue cheese, bacon, and radish. Try the sampler plate for two ("Taste of the Q") for a bit of ribs, sausage, chicken, pulled pork, and beef. Fried chicken is also on the menu (Mon night and Sun only), or visit on Tues night for the southern-fried catfish dinner. Open for lunch and dinner every day.

Big D Burgers, 1005 Silverado Trail, Napa, CA 94559; (707) 255-7188; www.bigdburgers.com; $. It has "burgers" in the name but there's much more on the menu: several salads, fish and chicken options, hot dogs, tacos, a protein plate for dieters, soups and chili, and ice cream in many flavors served in all the traditional ways, such as banana splits. The building's high-peaked roof with its goofy cartoon-like characters dates to the 1950s—as far back as folks can remember, this spot has always been a burger joint. Open daily from 11 a.m. to 8 p.m. (closing at 7 p.m. Sat and Sun).

Bistro Sabor, 1126 First St., Napa, CA 94559; (707) 252-0555; www.bistrosabor.com; $. Come for the food, stay for the hot salsa dancing on Saturday nights. This is an informal eatery, where you order at the counter from a hand-lettered menu board. Street food from Latin America is the prevailing cuisine, such as churros and *pupusas,* salmon ceviche tostadas, pan-seared salmon, chicken posole, fresh tropical fruit salads, and made-to-order tacos stuffed with roasted vegetables or seafood or carnitas. As many as 20 Mexican, local, and imported beers are available, as well as the Ceja family's boutique wines and sake (check out the Ceja wine tasting room just a few doors away at 1248 First St.). After Saturday night dinner, with a partner or without, you're welcome to dance the merengue, *cumbia,* and *bachata* into the wee hours to Latin music. (A complimentary dance lesson is offered at 10 p.m.) The music and the menu are both served late, with no cover charge. Open Tues through Sat for lunch and dinner—and to 1:30 a.m. on Fri and Sat nights (closed Sun and Mon).

Boon Fly Cafe, 4048 Carneros/Sonoma Hwy. (Hwy. 12/121), Napa, CA 94559; (707) 299-4880; www.thecarnerosinn.com; $$. Where did the name come from? Boon Fly was an early 19th-century pioneer who envisioned planting vineyards and orchards in the Carneros region. Once a haymaker, Boon Fly came west from Missouri as a wagon-train leader and eventually settled nearby. I'm betting that Boon Fly could not have envisioned the grub this cafe turns out, from the delectable Baker's Dozen doughnuts and the *chilaquiles* (typically eggs with tortillas and salsa) for breakfast, to the assorted flatbreads and daily specials for dinner. The cuisine is "modern rustic based on the agricultural heritage of the region"—which can mean a frequently changing menu using the best locally sourced ingredients available. The cafe is in the Carneros Inn resort, so watch for the red barnlike building along this fast-moving highway—that's the entrance. Boon Fly Cafe is open all day, every day, from 7 a.m. to 9 p.m.

Bounty Hunter Wine Bar & Smokin' BBQ, 975 First St., Napa, CA 94559; (707) 226-3976; www.bountyhunterwinebar.com; $$. Restaurant, wine-tasting bar, or wine shop—Bounty Hunter is all three. It began as a mail-order and online business for serious wine collectors, then moved into this space on First Street primarily as a wine shop selling rare vintages. At least 40 wines by the glass are poured, and as many as 400 bottles are on the wine list. It's also a great place for a meal to go with the wine. The signature dish at Bounty Hunter is beer-can chicken: a nearly full can of Tecate beer goes into the cavity of the chicken, the chicken stands up on the can in the oven, and is slowly steamed by the beer and roasted to perfection. (I've done this countless times on my backyard Weber grill—it's delish.) Speaking of beer, the restaurant also serves artisan brews, as well as Guinness on tap. Other food choices are Kobe beef sliders, an enormous 40-ounce rib eye steak, a daily sea-food special, several sandwiches and salads, and wine-bar snacks such as goat cheese and olives. Serving lunch and dinner daily, Bounty Hunter is one of the few places open late for a meal in downtown Napa, usually until midnight on weekends.

Ca' Momi Enoteca, 610 First St., Napa, CA 94559 (in the Oxbow Public Market); (707) 257-4992; www.camomi.com; $. The cuisine here is authentic Italian—obsessively so, as their motto proclaims. Using organic ingredients to make classic Neapolitan-style pizzas pulled from the wood-burning oven, the pies are sliced into quarters for folding in half the traditional Italian way. Ca' Momi's menu changes frequently, but salads, pastries, and other Italian dishes, with many of the ingredients sourced from other vendors in Oxbow Market, are always available. Try something from the *pasticceria,* too—*crostate* and *crostatine de frutta, baci di dama, zaetti, cantucci,* and biscotti. Ca' Momi has their own line of wines as well, with a 2007 Napa Valley Cabernet Sauvignon recently winning double-gold honors at the San Francisco International Wine Competition. Open daily 9 a.m. to 9 p.m.

Carpe Diem Wine Bar, 1001 Second St., Napa, CA 94559; (707) 224-0800; www.carpediemwinebar.com; $$. It's a wine bar, and also a restaurant. Order one of the more than 40 wines by glass (or a draft beer) and dip into the crispy deep-fried green olives filled with herbed goat cheese and crusted in panko crumbs. Move on to the artisanal cheese and *salumi* plate, or try the ostrich burger, the "Quack 'n' Cheese" (duck confit with caramelized onions and toasted bread crumbs in a three-cheese blend), or the Cabernet-braised short-rib sliders. Many of the ingredients are produced locally, including potato buns from Alexis Baking Company nearby.

Because it's also a wine bar, the staff can recommend just the right varietals for each course. Open Tues through Sat for happy hour (4 to 6 p.m.) and dinner.

Crossroad Chicken, (707) 280-3868; www.crossroadchix.com. Right inside the truck, this mobile vendor has a wood-fired oven that makes the large chicken and mozzarella sandwich extra tasty. Other choices could be green curry-coconut soup with chicken, a pulled-pork sandwich, or a smoked salmon sandwich with side salads. Chicken and dumplings or chicken hominy might also be on the menu. The Rancho Gordo heirloom bean chili is a steal at $4.95—see Rancho Gordo's listing in the Specialty Stores & Markets category.

Dim Sum Charlie's, (707) 815-2355; www.dimsum charlies.com. Generally located at 728 First St. in Napa, this food truck can also be found motoring around the region to serve at special events. In addition to many variations of dim sum (meat- or veggie-filled dumplings), the truck ladles up noodles in a choice of broth and with a few add-ins, such as a steamed farm-fresh egg or a braised duck leg.

Filippi's Pizza Grotto, 645 First St., Napa, CA 94559; (707) 254-9700; www.realcheesepizza.com. $. Kitty-corner from the Oxbow Public Market is Filippi's, consistently baking great pizza pie for many years. Filippi's is a California chain, based in San Diego and with 13 locations around the state. The Filippi family has been in the restaurant business for more than 50 years, and the grottos are run by the grandsons, granddaughters, great-grandsons and -granddaughters—and even the great-greats—of the original founders. The pizza menu is substantial and traditional, and includes some special combinations, too. Pasta is also available: spaghetti with meatballs or sausage, beef or cheese ravioli, lasagna, and complete dinners, such as veal or eggplant parmigiana, cheese manicotti, and fettuccine with chicken and artichokes. The decor is also traditional, from the red-checkered tablecloths to the Chianti bottles hanging overhead. Open daily for lunch and dinner.

Fish Story, 790 Main St., Napa, CA 94559; (707) 251-5600; www .fishstorynapa.com; $$$. Take note of the whimsical squid sculpture as you enter through the tiny courtyard at the front door. It sets the tone for the dining experience to come, including the interesting fishing lure decor hanging in the main dining room. Fish Story is part of the Lark Creek Restaurant Group, which operates high-end eateries in several California locations and also in Las Vegas. So it's corporate, yes, but that's not always a bad thing. Many standard seafood and fish dishes are on the menu, but this is not Red Lobster. "Towers" of seafood with condiments start small for two and get huge (the Moby Dick) for a group. Three types of Louie salads, smoked salmon deviled eggs, rock-cod ceviche, "old school" entrees prepared with traditional methods, and "new school" plates (including trout done two ways) are staples. Carnivores can order chicken, steak, and hamburgers, and the seasonal side dishes are extra. Vegan and vegetarian items can be prepared gluten-free. Serving lunch and dinner daily.

Gott's Roadside Tray Gourmet, 644 First St., Napa, CA 94559 (next to the Oxbow Public Market); (707) 224-6900; www.gottsroad side.com; $. Gott's was once known as Taylor's Refresher (and that sign still stands on the highway at the St. Helena location), but a legal dispute forced the recent name change. At either location in Napa Valley (the original in St. Helena, or this one next to Oxbow Market) you stand in line to order and are notified when your food is ready (with a vibrating pager at the Oxbow location). There's lots of outdoor seating, and the turnover of tables is frequent. Gott's throws together heaping, messy, three- and four-napkin burgers you can pair with four types of fries. Pick from several salads, hot dogs, and other sandwiches such as a BLT, turkey burger, veggie burger, and four chicken choices. The ahi tuna burger is a local favorite. Beer and Napa Valley wines are also served. Whenever possible, Gott's uses recyclable, renewable and compostable packaging. (A third Gott's is located in San Francisco's Ferry Building Marketplace.) Open daily for lunch and dinner.

Grace's Table, 1400 Second St., Napa, CA 94559; (707) 226-6200; www.gracestable.com; $$. With a "global kitchen" focus, Grace's Table takes its inspiration from many cuisines. Ask for the iron-skillet cornbread, which comes with lavender-honey butter, then the pear salad with wild arugula, candied walnuts, goat cheese, and tri-pepper *gastrique*. The chef's idea of surf-and-turf might be to combine the hanger steak frites with ahi tuna, garnished with bordelaise sauce. Other entrees could be cassoulet, pappardelle bolognese, and pork osso buco. The sweet finish may be a Valencia orange and Meyer lemon sorbet. Breakfast includes *chilaquiles*  (scrambled eggs with tortillas, ham, *pico de gallo,* and lime crème fraîche), or salmon gravlax on toasted bagels with cream cheese and capers. Grace's Table is only a short minute's walk to the Uptown Theater, so it makes a convenient pre-show stop for an appetizer or dinner. Open daily for breakfast, lunch, and dinner.

Highway 29 Cafe, 101 Cafe Ct., American Canyon, CA 94503; (707) 224-6303; $. Counter seat or a table? As an all-American diner serving breakfast and lunch, this cafe south of Napa at the north end of American Canyon can't be beat. The portions are generous, with flapjacks as big as Frisbees and a five-egg vegetarian omelette, if your heart can stand it. When the flea market is going on next door, parking can be challenging, but otherwise it's not a problem. After you've been on the gourmet trail for a few days, crispy hash browns and huge helpings of biscuits and gravy will probably hit the spot. Open daily for breakfast and lunch.

In-N-Out Burger, 820 Imola Ave., Napa, CA 94599; (800) 786-1000; www.in-n-out.com; $. On the West Coast, this California-based burger chain is legendary, dating back to 1948. Now, with more than 200 In-N-Outs in California alone (and several more in Arizona, Nevada, Utah, and Texas), you'll find one not too far from wherever you roam in the Golden State. Known for long lines at the drive-through (I know, it's not green), In-N-Out has millions of fans—and some true fanatics who wait all night for a new location to open its door so they can be the first customers in line. The posted menu is small: burgers, fries, shakes, and sodas. Yet there are some off-menu choices as well, once known only to the ravenous devotees of this fast food. The "not-so-secret" options are now available to anyone who asks. These include even larger burgers than you see on the board (with two, three, or even four beef patties and up to four cheese slices on one sandwich), a grilled cheese sandwich, and a burger wrapped in lettuce instead of a bun. A common design gimmick at most In-N-Out locations is the palm trees crossed to form an X. It's a long story, having to do with the late founder's love for the movie *It's a Mad Mad Mad Mad World*. Only in California! Open daily for lunch and dinner (to 1:30 a.m. on Fri and Sat).

Kitchen Door, 610 First St., Napa, CA 94559 (in the Oxbow Public Market); (707) 226-1560; www.kitchendoornapa.com; $. Touted more as a casual gathering spot than the newest foodie hangout, Kitchen Door opened to great anticipation in spring 2011. Chef-Owner Todd Humphries has had a long and respected career in the upscale restaurant industry in New York, San Francisco, and most recently in Napa Valley. His partner in this latest venture, Richard Miyashiro, was an executive in a multiple-restaurant empire in San Francisco and the Valley. They've teamed up to strip down haute cuisine and lower the prices, too, doing away with servers, tablecloths, and the need for reservations—cafeteria-style. You order at the counter, select your seat (consider making friends at the community tables), and Todd, Richard, or someone else on the staff delivers the food. Most items on the menu are well under $20. The wood-burning rotisserie and grill are continually churning out flatbreads, chicken, burgers, short ribs, salmon steak, and roast duck. Save room for the sweet stuff, like cookies, bread pudding, panna cotta, and ice cream. Kitchen Door is kid-friendly, and there's a "family meal" menu option that changes frequently. Open for lunch and dinner daily.

Mark's the Spot, (707) 226-7768; www.marks thespottruck.com. Keeping it simple, this food truck fries up a delicious chicken slider with a bit of peppered aioli inside a brioche bun. A burger, hot dog, barbecued brie with caramelized apple and red onion jam, turkey chili, seasonal salads and soups, and French toast on a stick are usually available, too. You can spot the truck by the big red circle on the side. Check the website for the truck's lunch and dinner locations, which can change with the seasons and the farmers' market schedules.

Mary's Pizza Shack, 3085 Jefferson St., Napa, CA 94559; (707) 257-3300; www.maryspizzashack.com; $. Even with 17 locations in northern California, the Sonoma County–based Mary's Pizza Shack doesn't scrimp on quality and consistency. If you order the spaghetti and meatball ("the size of a baseball") at the Napa location, it will be the same delicious dish at the downtown Santa Rosa restaurant. With a love for cooking, the late Mary Fazio opened her first pizzeria in 1959 in the town of Boyes Hot Springs near Sonoma, paying just $60 for the monthly rent. Popularity soared, a larger "shack" became necessary, and even more locations followed through the years. The Fazio family continues to operate the restaurants, from in-laws to grandchildren to great-grandchildren. The pizza is well-loved by the locals, yet the pasta options are also remarkable: spaghetti, ravioli, rotini, penne, bow ties, lasagna, gnocchi, linguine, and tortellini. Half-orders are available, too, for lighter appetites, and the calzones are large enough to feed two. Everything is made from scratch—no frozen dough or canned sauces. One of the best deals going is a bowl of thick minestrone with a Mary's Salad (crisp greens with eggs, mozzarella, beets, salami, and three-bean salad on top) for $6.50. The great flavors rival those found in much pricier restaurants. All Mary's Pizza Shacks are family-friendly and comfortable, and several even have a full bar. The Napa location serves wine and beer only (with happy hour from 3 to 6 p.m. weekdays). Open daily for lunch and dinner.

Mini Mango Thai Bistro, 1408 Clay St., Napa, CA 94559; (707) 226-8886; www.minimangonapa.com; $. This small eatery in downtown Napa serves Thai comfort food with California influences, including shared family plates. The calamari and papaya salads are excellent, along with the "8 Elements Wrap"—romaine lettuce leaves filled with grilled prawns, spinach, diced ginger, lime, shallot, and peanuts. A touch of roasted coconut–palm sugar sauce on top of each lettuce wrap adds an extra dimension of flavor. A pad thai combo is available, as are samosas, chicken-coconut soup, pot stickers, honey-barbecued pork, corn fritters, and much more. The service is attentive, and the food delivered quickly. Try to score a patio table if the weather is agreeable. Open daily for lunch and dinner.

Napa General Store, 540 Main St., Napa, CA 94559; (707) 259-0762; www.napageneralstore.com; $. If you're near the Napa Mill complex anyway, shopping or just walking around, duck into the General Store for a satisfying breakfast or lunch. When you first stroll in, it seems more like a gift shop, with jewelry, clothing, purses, a few kitchen and decor items, and wine accessories and wine posters for sale. (There's also a wine tasting bar.) But go on back to the cafe (starting at 8 a.m.) to pry your eyes open with coffee, huevos rancheros, or brioche French toast. Lunch fare might be two different types of pizza, Chinese chicken salad, clay-pot chicken, a barbecued pork sandwich, and a Greek salad. This dog-friendly eatery also has an outdoor patio overlooking the Napa River. Open daily for breakfast and lunch (closing at 4 p.m.).

Nation's Giant Hamburgers & Great Pies, 1441 Third St., Napa, CA 94559; (707) 252-8500; www.nationsrestaurants.com; $. The motto here is "big taste, large portions, huge difference." Standard breakfast fare is served in the morning, and at lunch it's traditional burgers. Also a chili burger, salmon burger, grilled cheese sandwich, chili dog, and ice cream shakes and sundaes. Don't forget the pies—in classic flavors, they are available by the slice or can be wrapped whole to go. The round building is distinctive, resembling a UFO at the corner of Third and School Streets. Open from 6 a.m. daily and closing late (11 p.m. Sun through Thurs, and 1 a.m. on weekends).

Neela's, 975 Clinton St., Napa, CA 94559; (707) 226-9988; www.neelasnapa.com; $$. Owner Neela Paniz established her reputation in southern California as operator of the popular Bombay Cafe in Los Angeles. Moving to Napa in 2008, she opened this much-welcome restaurant offering contemporary Indian food (a type of cuisine that had been lacking in Napa for some time). Neela taught herself to cook in her aunt's kitchen, from her family's cook in India, and from watching Julia Child on television. Small plates are available at Neela's, such as shrimp samosas or *rassols,* and medium presentations like lamb kebab sliders and *keema pao.* There are hearty tandoor specialties and curries, too. On Wednesday night, Neela's offers a 3-course vegetarian tasting menu, and Indian high tea is served on Saturday and Sunday afternoon. Open daily for lunch and dinner (closed Mon).

Norman Rose Tavern, 1401 First St., Napa, CA 94559; (707) 258-1516; www.normanrosenapa.com; $$. With a clubby feel, this restaurant is usually busy at peak times, so try to go during a slower hour. The "elevated" pub-type food is imaginative, and there's much to pick from. Their idea of bangers and mash is Caggiano bratwurst with sherry-roasted onions and red-skin mashed potatoes. A cheeseburger, lamb burger, snapper sandwich, buttermilk fried-chicken sandwich, or a gourmet grilled cheese sandwich will chase the hunger away. Wash it all down with one of the brews on an extensive list of beers by the bottle or on tap, as well as a big assortment of local and regional wines. Local food purveyors make appearances on the menu, including Five Dot Ranch beef and Fatted Calf Charcuterie for the meat, and Alexis Baking Company for breads. Norman Rose Tavern is located in what the locals call the new "west end" district of downtown Napa, which means the more prosperous stretch of First Street. Open for lunch and dinner daily.

Oenotri, 1425 First St., Napa, CA 94559; (707) 252-1022; www .oenotri.com; $$. The popularity of *salumi* exploded over the past couple of years, and it's restaurants such as Oenotri that led the way. The name of the restaurant is pronounced "oh-NO-tree," which translates to "vine cultivators." While many restaurants in Napa Valley serve Tuscan-inspired Italian cuisine, Oenotri focuses more on the flavors of southern Italy, with more fresh fish and

vegetables as key ingredients instead of the rich cheeses and heavier sauces found on other menus. The separate menu for *salumi* (all house-made) is varied, and a chef's selection of 6 or 10 choices is offered. On the main menu is pizza (including a version with wild nettles and cream), several antipasti and pasta choices, and main courses such as northern halibut with grilled asparagus and a roasted brace of quail with *fregula*. The two owner-chefs, Curtis Di Fede and Tyler Rodde, worked together at a restaurant in Oakland before deciding to join forces in this recently opened venture in Napa. Dinner is served daily.

Papa Joe's Pizza, 1121 Lincoln Ave., Napa, CA 94558; (707) 255-6525; www.papajoespizzaca.com; $. Everybody has a favorite pizza. It all depends on where you live, how you like your crust (thick, thin, or thinner), and what you prefer to have heaped onto your pie. No pizzeria can please all of the people all of the time, but Papa Joe's comes pretty close. The usual basic pizzas and gourmet options are here, along with the build-your-own option. Some die-hard pizza fiends might think that shrimp and artichoke hearts have no place on a pizza, but, dude, this is California. Look for the big "Lincoln Plaza" sign on the building—Papa Joe's is the business on the left. Open daily for lunch and dinner, with delivery available.

Pearl, 1339 Pearl St., Napa, CA 94559; (707) 224-9161; www.therestaurantpearl.com; $$$. The restaurant is sort of hidden in plain sight, on an awkward corner in downtown Napa that many drivers cruise past because they are, well, confused. Ongoing construction nearby on the Napa River flood project has made finding Pearl a bit more challenging because of off-and-on closed streets, but it's worth the effort to seek out. The locals love this place, and for good reason. It's part oyster bar—with the bivalves flavored several ways—and a great meeting place. Order the roast duck with pear-and-ginger chutney, or the double-thick pork chop in an apple-Dijon brine. Simple meat loaf gets a makeover at Pearl, accented with fennel sausage and accompanied by Brooklyn-style red gravy. One of the signature dishes is ginger-marinated flank steak soft tacos, served in housemade tortillas. Open Tues through Sat for lunch and dinner.

Red Hen Cantina, 4175 Solano Ave., Napa, CA 49558; (707) 255-8125; www.redhencantina.com; $. This is a reliable place for a good south-of-the-border meal and a tasty margarita. Check out the interesting photo gallery in the bar before you take your seat. While there are some elements of the usual Mexican restaurant decor, Red Hen has dark wood interior, plush booths, and green plants, too. The large patio area has a huge fountain, and there's also a small video arcade for the kids. Try one of the specialties, such as mole enchiladas or the *carne asada a la tampiquena:* grilled tri-tip resting on onions, peppers, guacamole, cheese, and *pico de gallo.* Prefer breakfast for lunch? Red Hen can plate up a hearty mound of huevos rancheros or chorizo con huevos, as well as several varieties of two-egg omelettes, until 4 p.m. There are even some soda fountain treats such as root beer floats and banana splits. Vegetarian options are available, and straight-up hamburgers too. Look for the big red hen on top of the building. Open daily for lunch and dinner.

Ristorante Allegria, 1026 First St., Napa, CA 94559; (707) 254-8006; www.ristoranteallegria.com; $$. Take note of the building—formerly a bank, it's nearly a century old. The restaurant makes great use of the 35-foot ceilings and what was once the bank's vault, now a private dining room for up to 10 people. You have to admit, the place has atmosphere. When the weather is fine, ask for a patio table. Allegria does a superb job of presenting fine Italian cuisine with a California twist here and there. There's plenty of pasta and polenta, along with traditional fare such as veal scaloppine. Allegria also offers a "lunch box" menu: for $15, you can select from a choice of four entrees, three salads, and sorbet. Open for lunch and dinner daily.

Small World Cafe, 932 Coombs St., Napa, CA 94559; (707) 224-7743; www.worldcafenapa.com; $. The proprietor is a native Israeli who opened this small establishment to offer delicious recipes that have been in his family for generations. Count on vegetable pitas, meat pitas, falafel platters, lamb gyros, hummus, and fresh baklava—made daily from fresh ingredients. Traditional hamburgers, breakfast omelettes, and fruit smoothies are on the hand-lettered menu, too. This is a

favorite of locals. Open 6 days a week (closed Sun), for breakfast, lunch, and dinner.

Squeeze Inn, 3383 Solano Ave., Napa, CA 94558; (707) 257-6880; www.squeezeinnhamburgers.com; $. I hope you love cheese on your burger, because Squeeze Inn smothers its "Squeezeburger" with the stuff. While the burger is grilling, a huge handful of shredded cheese is dumped on top. It melts like lava over the burger and what spills onto the grill is also fried, creating what the owners refer to as a "cheese skirt." The Food Network's *Diners, Drive-Ins & Dives* program graphically demonstrated how it's done at the Sacramento location, one of four Squeeze Inns in northern California. The most expensive item on the menu is a steak sandwich. Unlike typical fast-food burger joints, this one can sell you a beer, and happy hour is from 4 to 6 p.m. Open for lunch and dinner Mon through Sat.

UVA Trattoria Italiana, 1040 Clinton St., Napa, CA 94559; (707) 255-6646; www.uvatrattoria.com; $$. A favorite of locals, UVA has live music 5 nights a week, generally light jazz and blues, without a cover charge. The restaurant has a neighborhood supper-club feel, spacious but intimate, too—suitable for any occasion and all ages. Check out the old photos of sports figures, movie stars, and even some Napa residents while you browse through the menu. Traditional pizzas, pastas, and steaks show some "California cuisine" influences, such as the pan-roasted sea bass over roasted leeks, garlic, and roasted tomatoes; the ravioli d'Erbè (ricotta and herb-filled ravioli with crispy sage, pecorino, and brown butter);

and the prosciutto-stuffed organic quail over fresh porcini mushroom risotto. Open daily (except Mon) for lunch and dinner.

Zinsvalley, 1106 First St., Napa, CA 94559; (707) 224-0695; www .zinsvalley.com; $$. "Inspired American cuisine" is the draw at Zinsvalley, with dishes such as steak frites and coconut yellow curry sharing the menu with chicken piccata and linguine. For starters, the spring rolls, calamari, rosemary flatbread, and smoked-salmon pizza are usually featured. Happy hour gets going early at Zinsvalley, as if you're on Central Standard Time—Monday through Friday from 2 to 6 p.m. (and all night on Wednesday). In town on a Tuesday night? Order the hamburger with fries at half-price. Thursday nights are for $6 martinis. There's a late-night menu, too (10 p.m. to midnight every night) of sliders, pizza, shrimp, wings, and cheese. Open daily for lunch and dinner, and for Sunday brunch starting at 10 a.m.

ZuZu, 829 Main St., Napa, CA 94559; (707) 224-8555; www.zuzu napa.com; $$. Tapas rule at this restaurant, California style. With seasonal and local ingredients, and organic when possible, the small plates might include the seafood ceviche of the day, rabbit *rillettes*, shaved artichoke, chicken croquettes, Sonoma Coast lamb chops, Niman Ranch pork meatballs, mussels with chiles, Sardinian couscous, and much more. Ask for the grilled octopus if you don't see it on the menu— Chef Angela Tamura might be able to accommodate your wishes. The wine list features more than 25 wines by the glass—a generous number, compared to many restaurants—and lots

The Origin of "Napa"

Ever wonder where the word "Napa" comes from, and what it means? There has been much debate over the past century about the word's derivation, and it's been translated several ways: grizzly bear, motherland, fish, and house. Most experts seem to lean toward "house," from the Patwin word "napo." The Patwin were native inhabitants of northern California for hundreds of years before the white man arrived, and one of their villages was called Napato.

Whatever it means, "Napa" evokes a certain feeling or lifestyle, and it's become a popular name for restaurants elsewhere who want to cash in on that Napa vibe. There's a Napa Valley Grille in New Jersey, the Napa Grille Urban Wine Bar in Texas, and two restaurants in Reno with Napa in their names: Bistro Napa and Cafe Napa. The Napa Restaurant can be found in Las Vegas, and another with the same name in Orlando.

Napa Rose is the restaurant at the Grand Californian Hotel at Disneyland in Anaheim. The Napa Wine Bar & Restaurant operates in Massachusetts, and Napa Cafe has been serving customers in Memphis, Tennessee, since 1998. And there's more: Napa & Company restaurant is in Connecticut; Napa Grille & Wine Den can be found in snowy Ontario, Canada; and the Napa River Grill in Louisville, Kentucky, promotes a wine country–themed menu.

Awareness of Napa as a desirable destination isn't limited to America. Next time you're in London, reserve a table at the Napa Restaurant in Chiswick Moran Hotel on Chiswick High Road for "modern British food." Going to Cairo? Check out the California cuisine served at the elegant Napa Grill in the Fairmont Hotel Nile City, with tables overlooking the Nile River.

of bottles under $30. ZuZu has an inexpensive, house-blended sangria, too. Open for lunch and dinner Mon through Fri, and dinner on Sat and Sun.

Specialty Stores & Markets

Alexis Baking Company, 1517 Third St., Napa, CA 94559; (707) 258-1827; www.alexisbakingcompany.com. Known commonly as ABC, this is a bakery, cafe, and catering business. Operating for more than 25 years, ABC was a wholesale bakery first, then branched out into retail and later added breakfast and lunch, too. All the standard bakery items can be found here: French pastries, 10 types of muffins, cookies galore, scones, coffee cakes and pound cakes, and brownies. The savory cafe fare leans to burritos and omelettes for breakfast to soup and salad specials for lunch. ABC also puts together tasty box lunches with prior notice (and delivery is available). These come in two sizes, for one or two persons, with three focaccia sandwiches to choose from, a selection of side salads, cookies or other sweet treats, and the napkins and utensils you'll need for your picnic.

Anette's Chocolates and Ice Cream Factory, 1321 First St., Napa, CA 94559 (main location and factory), (707) 252-4228; and 610 First St., Napa, CA 94559 (in the Oxbow Public Market); www .anettes.com. Peanut brittle made with beer, truffles infused with red or white wines, chocolate bars with creamy, dreamy fillings—a huge assortment of chocolate treats is available at this shop in downtown Napa (and its other location about five blocks away in the Oxbow Market). The main store is where the innovations and the manufacturing take place. Anette Madsen and her brother, Brent Madsen, have been working together for many years, bringing forth fine chocolate products and their own luscious ice cream on this site. That includes chocolate wine sauces for use in cooking or for drizzling over desserts, boxed truffles and chews in all sizes, heart-shaped chunks of chocolate, and cans of milk-chocolate or dark-chocolate disks. I can personally recommend the beer peanut brittle (available with or without a touch of chile), the Chardonnay peanut brittle, the Kentucky bourbon peanut brittle, and the dark-chocolate and Cabernet truffle bar. It's pretty difficult to pick a favorite in this store, but you'll enjoy trying.

Butter Cream Bakery and Diner, 2297 Jefferson St., Napa, CA 94559; (707) 255-6700; www.buttercreambakery.com. Dating to 1948, Butter Cream built its reputation on thousands and thousands of delicious doughnuts. That eventually led to pies and bread, then cakes were added into the mix. You can find Butter Cream's products in area grocery stores, but it's more fun to see all the choices right at the source (note: their most popular treats are maple bars and apple fritters). Classic diner food is also served, with breakfast available all day, every day. Try the turkey salad on Butter Cream's own croissant, or the soup of the day (along with chili, during the rainy season). The half-pound hamburgers are reasonably priced, served on the bakery's own burger buns. Shaking up the burger menu is the Bobbi burger (the half-pound patty smothered with grilled onions and mustard on grilled muffin bread), or the black-bean burger, served with pepper jack cheese, salsa, and guacamole. Go for the full treatment by adding a milk shake, mocha shake, or root-beer float. Desserts, of course, are made in-house, so don't leave without a sticky bun or a napoleon.

Still owned by the Closs family that first established the business, the pink-and-white striped building is easy to spot. The diner and bakery both open early every day, at 5:30 a.m.

Fatted Calf Charcuterie, 644-C First St., Napa, CA 94559 (near the Oxbow Public Market); (707) 256-3684; www.fattedcalf.com. (Vegetarians, you can skip over this listing.) *Chicharrónes,* anyone? Fatted Calf makes small batches of cured meats that are aged using traditional methods. That includes pâtés, salami, prosciutti, confits, sausage, and by-products such as their popular pork-rind snack. Organic ingredients are sourced and used as much as possible, including pasture-raised pork, grass-fed beef, and locally raised duck, lamb, and game hens. The store's inventory is varied and delicious, from all-beef hot dogs to pork terrine with porcini and bacon. Check out the deli case with sandwiches, pasta, cheese, and more. This location (there's another in San Francisco) also sells locally produced olive oil and pasta. You can bring your empty olive oil bottle back in again and again for refilling, too. Fatted Calf also conducts regular classes in curing and preparing meat (see Learn to Cook in this chapter).

Kara's Cupcakes, 610 First St., Napa, CA 94559 (in the Oxbow Public Market); (707) 258-2253; www.karascupcakes.com. The cupcake phenomenon shows no signs of flaming out—yet. Kara's is a 6-store northern California chain that makes use of mostly local ingredients, as well as environmentally friendly packaging, utensils, and bags that are recyclable and compostable. Feel better now about pigging out on sweets? I hope so, because the Meyer lemon and passion fruit cupcake is worth it, or the chocolate raspberry. Owner Kara Lind's dad was a dentist, so she had to sneak sugary treats as a kid. Now she operates a whole empire devoted to them. Besides the small cakes, larger cakes in cupcake flavors are for sale—big enough to serve eight hungry dessert fans.

Michoacan Natural Ice Cream, 3085 Jefferson St., Napa, CA 94558; (707) 265-7919. Owned and operated locally, Michoacan (named after a state in Mexico) has 22 flavors of ice cream that are made on-site with real fruit—no artificial flavorings. So the strawberry ice cream is loaded with strawberries, and the 17 popsicle flavors are the real deal, too. Yet it's the exotic choices that are bringing in the customers: *chongo* (imagine if flan were ice cream), rum and raisin, *cajeta,* and Mexican chocolate are available, along with more traditional flavors. Save room for a guava popsicle or a *mangonada,* a frosty treat that combines fresh mango and ice.

Model Bakery, 644 First St., Bldg. B, Napa, CA 94559 (adjacent to the Oxbow Public Market); (707) 259-1128; www.themodelbakery .com. You can't walk into the Model Bakery and not walk out with a couple of the incomparable English muffins. Nothing like those pre-packaged grocery store hockey pucks, Model Bakery's English muffins are whole (not split), as light as air, and so melt-in-your-mouth delicious that they don't even require jam or butter to enhance the experience. You can also get slices of pizza, a daily salad selection, some fresh prepared sandwiches, and soup. Model Bakery's main store is in St. Helena (see that chapter), and that's where most of the baking is done. The Napa location bakes loaves of bread, but most everything else is brought in fresh every morning from the Upvalley location.

Napa Valley Coffee Roasting Company, 948 Main St., Napa, CA 94559; (707) 224-2233; www.napavalleycoffee.com. Small, quiet, and staffed by friendly baristas—who could ask for more in a good coffee shop? The beans are from Indonesia, Africa, and the Americas for variety, and are roasted in small 20-pound batches almost every night to ensure freshness. Order a latte or cappuccino or just straight black coffee. Wouldn't it go down better with a biscotto, muffin, cookie, or doughnut? There's usually an assortment of interesting reading material strewn about, if you forgot to bring your own. Napa Valley Coffee Roasting Company has a second location in St. Helena (see that chapter).

Napa Valley Kitchen Gallery, 952 School St., Napa, CA 94559; (707) 253-2828; www.nvkitchengallery.com. In 2011, the store's owner, Lynn Campagna, a longtime Napa resident and home cook, moved her inventory closer to downtown and the more concentrated foodie action (the store is now across from Napa's City Hall). With restaurant-quality products and brand names to choose from, the store attracts professional chefs as well as culinary hobbyists. Let your fingers do the walking through the Japanese and German knives, or the Victorinox line of blades. Expect cookware, tableware, and bakeware by Le Creuset, Mauviel, USA Pans, Emile Henry, Cuisinart, Jura Capresso, and more. At this new location Lynn has also added an olive-oil bar, exclusive hand towels and aprons made by a local artist, and an expanded selection of food. Future plans call for Lynn to conduct cooking classes on-site—check with her for the latest.

Osprey Seafood Market, 1014 Wine Country Ave., Napa, CA 94558; (707) 252-9120. Local restaurant chefs know all about this place, and probably wish you didn't. Osprey is a straightforward fish market, in business for more than a decade. On any given day your choices might be fresh lobsters, king salmon, oysters, soft-shell or

Dungeness crabs, skate wing, sand dabs, halibut, petrale sole, ahi tuna, swordfish, black cod, and trout. The staff can recommend how to cook your purchase, if you need some help in that department. Ask for the manager, Chris, who once cheffed himself.

Phat Salads and Wraps, (707) 363-9658; www.phatsalads.com. Wraps are the specialty of this mobile food vendor, with a choice of grilled chicken or steak and assorted other ingredients. Choose from a "New Yorker" to a "Classic Caesar" or one called "Simply Napa"— all veggie. Ask for your wrap to be "phat" and they will double the protein for an extra charge. This truck also serves a breakfast wrap until mid-morning, filled with scrambled eggs, cheese, and choice of meat.

Rancho Gordo New World Specialty Food, 1924 Yajome St., Napa, CA 94559; (707) 259-1935; www.ranchogordo.com. Thanks to the entrepreneurial and exceptionally likeable Steve Sando, Rancho Gordo is a huge online success, yet the business retains its small-city friendliness and commitment to the community at this storefront location in a largely residential neighborhood. The business has also been praised by big-time chefs such as Mario Batali and Emeril Lagasse. Dried heirloom beans, mostly grown in the nearby Delta region of the San Francisco Bay area, are the main event at Rancho Gordo, accounting for about 90 percent of the bean inventory. The remaining 10 percent comes from growers in Mexico, through a farming partnership Steve established called the Rancho

Gordo-Xoxoc Project. Beans with colorful names you've never heard of before are cleverly packaged in 1-pound cellophane bags, with the company's trademark woman-licking-her-lips graphic on each one. The beans are fresh, which is to say usually less than a year old from harvest to bag. That sounds positively prehistoric when talking about food, but consider this: bags of dried beans found on a typical grocery store shelf can be up to 10 years old. So the difference in freshness is remarkable, and you can taste it in every variety you simmer. A pound bag of Eye of the Goat or Yellow Eye combined with a half-pound of great ham hocks (and with a handful of chopped onion, a bay leaf, and a little bit of chopped carrot tossed in) will yield two separate meals of creamy beans, simmered in a slow-cooker or on low heat on the range top. Get addicted to Rancho Gordo beans and you'll also acquire some new culinary lingo, such as "pot liquor" (ask Steve to explain). The website has many recipes and tips for cooking the beans, and the store's staff can instruct you in the finer points, as well. While there, the large "touching beans" tub of loose beans of all types draws you in with a sign that reads: "Go ahead—you know you want to!" And so you sink your hands into the tub and start kneading away. Cookbooks, including Steve's own, are also for sale, along with Mexican chocolates, dried chiles, heirloom popcorn, spices, and dried prickly-pear cactus. Rancho Gordo's small store is a few blocks north of downtown Napa—look for the awning over the door. See Steve Sando's recipe for **Rancho Gordo's Posole Verde** on p. 227.

Ritual Coffee Roasters, 610 First St., Napa, CA 94559 (in the Oxbow Public Market); (707) 253-1190; www.ritualroasters.com. The Oxbow Public Market isn't a quiet haven for sipping coffee while you read the latest Deepak Chopra tome. Oxbow is usually bustling with activity and the sounds of food preparation and general commerce, even making conversation difficult at times. But if you're jonesing for some joe here, nobody does it better than Ritual Roasters. Serra Negro drip coffee, with a bit of cocoa sweetness, is available, and the espresso is a blend from several coffee-bean producers. There's usually a seasonal blend, such as Hibernator in winter, with tropical fruit flavors. Most afternoons, customers can take part in a "cupping" process that's similar to wine tasting. The baristas let you smell the beans whole, then ground, to compare the aromas. Hot water is then poured into the grounds for another round of aroma-sampling. After that the coffee is brewed for tasting and evaluation. Ritual's flagship store in San Francisco is where the roasting takes place, but bags of beans are rushed regularly to this Napa location, bearing a roasting date to prove they are truly fresh. Seating can be somewhat limited, as the jumble of tables and chairs in front of the counter might already be filled with people noshing on tacos or ice cream from nearby vendors. If the weather is agreeable, try the patio just outside that overlooks the Napa River.

Shackford's Kitchen Store, 1350 Main St., Napa, CA 94559; (707) 226-2132. Have you ever browsed in an old general store in a small town? Shackford's is a bit like one of those. Looking as if it's been there forever on a well-traveled street corner, Shackford's makes use of every inch of floor space, wall space, and counter space. The enormous inventory of food preparation equipment and utensils can't be described here adequately, but trust me, if you need something for cooking or baking, Shackford's has it. That includes replacement parts for many small home appliances, so you don't have to throw out your beloved countertop bread machine just because you (or maybe it was your husband) mysteriously lost the whirligig that slips down over the whatchamacallit, and without it the device is useless (I'm still in mourning). Shackford's probably stocks the whirligig, or can get it for you. A huge selection of cookbooks, kitchen linens, cutlery, canning supplies, and the ChefWorks designer line of chef's apparel will keep you occupied for hours. The store also offers professional knife and scissor sharpening.

Sift Cupcake & Dessert Bar, 3816 Bel Aire Plaza, Napa, CA 94558; (707) 240-4004; www.siftcupcakes.com. When she had difficulty finding creative cupcakes for her wedding in nearby Sonoma, the owner of Sift decided to go into business for herself, making the type of confections she knew customers would want: cupcakes, whoopie pies, frosting shots, profiteroles, macaroons, and ice cream sandwiches. Another Sift creation is cruffles—bite-sized morsels of cake and frosting blended together, then hand-dipped in chocolate. Sift also makes a cupcake based on a local brewery's Hairy Eyeball Beer. Being the big winner in the Food Network's *Cupcake Wars* in 2010 secured Sift's place in cupcake history. Their winning entry:

raspberry with Champagne buttercream frosting. Ask for it at this location or at Sift's two other stores in Sonoma County's Santa Rosa and Cotati. Sift also has a mobile cupcake truck, the Sifter, that can be rented for special events.

Soda Canyon Store, 4006 Silverado Trail, Napa, CA 94558; (707) 252-0285; www.sodacanyonstore.com. As you motor north on Silverado Trail after leaving the city of Napa behind, consider stopping at this roadside establishment with the brown awning, where the Trail meets Soda Canyon Road. It's a popular stop for locals who need to pick up a few groceries, but it also has a huge selection of fine wine, an espresso bar, full-service deli, picnic supplies, gifts, patio seating, and a shaded picnic area along the creek behind the store. The store can put together a box lunch with your choice of sandwich, side salad, a sweet treat, and a piece of fruit. They even wrap up the box with a ribbon for an extra touch of class. Need to cater an event? Soda Canyon Store can do that, too.

Sweetie Pies Bakery, 520 Main St., Napa, CA 94559; (707) 257-8817; www.sweetiepies.com. Like many small businesses, this one had humble beginnings, born in an apartment kitchen with a ridiculously tiny oven. Now it produces dozens of cookies, muffins, cakes, and other baked goods every day, and serves savory lunches, too. Try a gooey granola bar or a miniature Kahlua mousse cake, and be sure to ask about their pumpkin pie that was featured on *The Rachael*

Ray Show. The bakery is located at the historic Napa Mill complex along the Napa River. Take your treats right outside to nosh at one of the bright red bistro tables.

Three Twins Organic Ice Cream, 610 First St., Napa, CA 94559 (in the Oxbow Public Market); (707) 257-TWIN; www.threetwins icecream.com. Named for the twin brothers (and for the twin that one of the brothers married) who started the business, Three Twins prides itself on being a green business—from the creamy organic product that goes in your mouth to the compostable serving dishes you eat from that won't end up in a landfill. Besides dishing up cones and cups at three scoop shops in the San Francisco Bay Area, the company also sells wholesale tubs to many regional restaurants and grocery stores. The names of their exclusive flavors will have you salivating: strawberry je ne sais quoi (strawberry with a splash of balsamic vinegar); cookie jar (vanilla with three types of cookies); PBC3 (peanut butter cookie confetti crunch); and the chocolate project (over-the-top with you-know-what).

Tillerman Tea, 610 First St., Napa, CA 94559 (in the Oxbow Public Market); (707) 265-0200; www.tillermantea.com. Before hot tea became the new coffee in America, I was drinking it by the gallon. So when Tillerman Tea opened in the Oxbow Market, I was beside myself with glee. Maybe it's the brewing rituals, the pretty packaging, the bright red canisters, the mystique of the leaf, or the exotic aromas. It might even be the roasted pumpkin seeds coated in green tea, for cleansing the palate between tea tastes, that Tillerman offers to customers. Most of the tea sold here is from China, where proprietor David Campbell learned firsthand about the beverage and the growing of the tea. He previously worked in the wine industry for more than two decades, and understands and admires some of the similarities between tea and wine. A few Japanese and Taiwanese teas are also for sale. Tea tasting and instruction are offered, along with monthly workshops on tea appreciation. To get the full enjoyment from your tea, David sells books, infusers, and tea cups and tea pots to make the experience complete.

Tyler Florence Kitchen Essentials, 710 Main St., Napa, CA 94559; (707) 254-9977; www.tylerflorence.com. While Michael Chiarello's NapaStyle store in Yountville celebrates the gusto of Italian cooking, celebrity chef Tyler Florence's retail shop in the Riverfront complex has a breezier vibe, reminiscent of a corner store in a Paris neighborhood from simpler times. I almost expected a young Brigitte Bardot to stroll in. The blue-and-white awning beckons visitors into the bright and airy store, with Julia Child on the flat-screen monitor demonstrating how to clarify butter, surrounded by rows of Emile Henry tableware. Look up: those wine-barrel chandeliers overhead are *très* cool (and for sale). Fondle the seductive nonstick paring knives in pastel hues. Select a few French Lucite spoons and spatulas in retro shades. Grab a handful of heavy vintage silverware sold by the piece or the place setting. Don't forget a bag of old-fashioned barber-pole-style paper—paper!—drinking straws in different colors. Pantry items such as sauces, marinades, spices, salts, and olive oils are lined up with precision, many from the Tyler Florence food line. Tyler's signature cookware is also on the shelves, along with his cookbooks (ask store manager Jessica about having yours autographed). This store is slightly smaller than the chef's other retail outlet, located in Mill Valley in nearby Marin County.

Vallerga's Market, 3385 Solano Ave., Napa, CA 94558; (707) 253-2621; www.vallergas.com. Sure, you could pop into the nearest Safeway store, but why? Homegrown Vallerga's Market has been serving generations of Napans for more than 60 years and has never been more popular than it is today. Vallerga's has not only kept up with the times but has moved beyond what would be merely adequate for a typical chain grocer. That includes a fresh salad bar, a hot bar with comfort food (the menu changes nightly), and more organic produce than anywhere else in Napa. Much of it is hand-picked at San Francisco produce marts every night in the wee hours and brought back in time for the store's opening each morning. If you're exhausted and need a hot meal to take home or to your hotel room, a quick stop at Vallerga's is in order. The choices might be chicken cordon bleu or meat loaf one night, and stuffed pork roast and grilled salmon on another night. The green salads, fruit salads, and specialty salads can be customized from a huge selection of fresh toppings. Sides vary, too, so load up on fresh green beans, glazed carrots, roasted potatoes, or couscous. As a hometown business, Vallerga's is a true supporter of Napa's good causes, having donated thousands of dollars worth of merchandise down through the years to local events, clubs, and organizations.

Vintage Sweet Shoppe, 530 Main St., Napa, CA 94558; (707) 224-2986; www.vintagesweetshoppe.com. For 30 years, the owners of this store have been making like the Willy Wonkas of Napa Valley, developing and selling chocolate treats such as truffles in many incarnations, fudge, and much more. Taking chocolate mania many, many steps further, the business earns its "vintage" moniker by creating custom-made chocolate-coated bottles of fine wine—the ultimate wine-and-chocolate pairing. The bottle of Napa Valley wine is first shrink-wrapped, then slathered in approximately a half-pound of milk chocolate or dark chocolate (your choice), with the label still visible. When you're ready to enjoy the experience, begin peeling away the chocolate from the top and pull the cork. Take a bite of chocolate, a sip of wine, a little bit more chocolate, a bigger sip of wine—and so on and so on until both are gone. Sinfully good, no doubt about it. Vintage Sweet Shoppe is in the Napa Mill complex.

Whole Spice, 610 First St., Napa, CA 94559 (in the Oxbow Public Market); (707) 256-0700; www.wholespice.com. If it has anything to do with adding a dash of flavor to one dish or an entire meal, it's in a jar here and available for purchase in small quantities or large. The choices among the 300-plus stock of spices and herbs will make your head spin: curry powders of all kinds, a myriad of cinnamon and salt choices, dried chiles from low heat to molten lava, mushroom powders, paprikas—and so on. The owners, Ronit and Shuli Madmone, claim they learn from the chefs who stop by "as much as they learn from us." The Madmones grind their spices at a warehouse in nearby Petaluma, so the products are fresh. If you can't find what you're looking for (fennel pollen, for instance?), the Madmones can track it down and order it. Ask about their occasional cooking classes, and also storage tips for the herbs and spices you purchase.

Farmers' Markets & Farm Stands

Big Ranch Farms, 2046 Big Ranch Rd., Napa, CA 94558; (707) 224-0611; www.homecook.me/bigranchfarms. Mark Haberger is a busy farmer who grows fruits, vegetables, and heirloom tomatoes

Latino Markets on the Rise

Fruits with unfamiliar names such as mamey and cherimoya are neatly stacked in the produce section, while freshly baked *pan dulce* add color to the bakery department. Shopping in a Latino grocery store opens up a new world of eating and cooking possibilities, whether it's learning to use tomatillos or beef tongue in one recipe, or selecting just the right heat and flavor of dried chiles for another.

For the uninitiated, *pan dulce* are pastries eaten as a snack or for dessert, available in many shapes and flavors. Baked daily and usually a sell-out is the colorful and highly addictive *concha,* stenciled with pastel icing to resemble a seashell. Fresh mamey fruit is prized for its hints of almonds and chocolate, and is used for making mousse or ice cream. Cherimoya (also known as a custard apple) can be eaten raw or sliced into salads.

Sprinkled around Napa Valley, several well-stocked Latino markets dispense meat, produce, and baked goods that are nearly impossible to find at other grocery stores. They also attract customers on the go in search of freshly made,

that he sells at the farmers' markets in Napa, St. Helena, and Calistoga throughout the market season. He also sets up a produce stand in summer at the Big Ranch Road address, offering whatever is ready to eat: heirloom tomatoes, chard, kale, arugula, baby spinach, turnips, melons, corn, eggplants, and more. Mark says to authentic taqueria food. Here are some popular Latin markets in the Valley, listed from south to north:

Juanita Market & Taqueria, 1725 W. Imola Ave., Napa, CA 94559; (707) 254-9121.

La Morenita Market, 2434 Jefferson St., Napa, CA 94558; (707) 255-9068; www.lamorenitamarket.com.

La Tapatia Market, 504 Brown St., Napa, CA 94559; (707) 226-7587; www.latapatiamarket.com.

Mi Familia Market, 2565 Kilburn Ave., Napa, CA 94558; (707) 226-3954; www.mifamiliamarket.com.

Mi Favorita Market, 3385 California Blvd., Napa, CA 94558; (707) 255-2087.

La Luna Market & Taqueria, 1135 Rutherford Rd., Rutherford, CA 94573; (707) 963-3211.

Azteca Market, 789 Main St., St. Helena, CA 94574; (707) 963-4963.

Vallarta Market Carniceria y Taqueria, 1009 Foothill Blvd., Calistoga, CA 94515; (707) 942-8864.

expect some "flowery produce" at his farm stand, too, such as sunflowers, zinnias, and dahlias for sale. He grows much of the produce on 19 acres in neighboring Solano County (where the climate is better suited to warm-weather crops), and many of his fresh vegetables are used in Napa Valley restaurants, too.

Chef's Market, along First and Coombs Streets, Napa, CA 94559; (707) 257-0322; www.donapa.com. From May to August, on Thursday from 5 to 9 p.m., streets in downtown Napa are blocked off to become a party zone for showcasing food and wine. Fresh fruits and vegetables are abundant at the farm stands, as well as hot food stands and opportunities for wine tasting. Don't miss the chef's demonstrations, when two or more local chefs show how to make cucumber gazpacho, perhaps, or peanut butter and Oreo truffles. As a family-friendly market, the little ones have their own large area for kid activities (and some for their parents, too), such as face painting, arts and crafts, and a storyteller who leads the children in song. Count on two or three upbeat musical groups to provide entertainment on different stages, too. Plans were in place in spring 2011 for the food trucks listed in this chapter to be serving at the market along Randolph Street.

Clerici Ranch, 2224 Oak Knoll Ave., Napa, CA 94558; (707) 287-7414; www.clericiranch.wordpress.com, and on Facebook. Owned by the same family for more than 100 years, this farm is also known to locals as "that chicken ranch in Napa." The Clerici family raises two types of chickens, one for eggs and the other for meat. The owners have a symbiotic relationship with their fowl, raising only as many birds per acre as is ecologically feasible. No chemicals are used on the farm, and the chickens produce the natural fertilizer that is composted for the garden. Three acres are set aside for growing fruits and vegetables: green beans, onions, tomatoes, lettuce, chard, artichokes, and organic raspberries and strawberries—whatever will grow best, depending on the weather from year to year. Barbara Clerici sets out a farm stand along the road when there's enough produce to justify the need, and payment is usually by the honor system. Visitors are welcome to tour the ranch with advance notice if they want to see for themselves how the happy chickens are raised and cared for. Watch for updates on the ranch's Facebook page to order the freshly processed chickens—literally from farm to table—and a few dozen eggs, too.

Connolly Ranch, 3141 Browns Valley Rd., Napa, CA 94558; (707) 224-1894; www.connollyranch.org. The ranch is a nonprofit organization and real working farm that hosts field trips for schoolchildren and holds a couple of annual visiting days for everyone (it's not open to the public otherwise). Hands-on educational programs for young students are the focus, so they may learn to appreciate the benefits of healthful food, where it comes from, how it is grown, and how to prepare it. That includes a farm animal tour for kids to interact with sheep, goats, and chickens up close; tours that explore environmental history and early pioneer life; and a "dirt to dine" program that takes students into the garden to see sources of food in the ground, followed by the kids preparing a simple meal using some of those ingredients. Twice a year, in June and October, the farm is open for a few hours free for families to meet the livestock and enjoy refreshments. There are also occasional special fundraising events with guest chefs (Michael Chiarello, for example) cooking up a gourmet meal, with all proceeds poured back into the educational programs at the ranch.

D&S Produce and Wild Boar Farms at Stanly Lane Nursery, 3100 Golden Gate Dr., Napa, CA 94558; (707) 480-4479; www.ds-produce.com, and www.wildboarfarms.com. In spring, be prepared to see more varieties of heirloom tomato plants here than anywhere else. Brad Gates of Wild Boar Farms is the tomato master, and he offers free tomato planting classes every Saturday beginning in April, until the plants are all sold, usually by the end of May. Then the seasonal produce stand opens in early June with almost every fresh vegetable you could ask for. During summer, the produce stand is open Wednesday through Sunday from 10 a.m. to 6 p.m., and winds down for the season at the end of October with a pumpkin patch. The complex just off the junction of Highways 29 and 12/121 also includes the Stanly Lane Marketplace and Olive Mill, a year-round retail store selling loads of foodie gifts, and with historic pictures of the region on the walls. Choose from locally made chocolates and olive oil, balsamic and wine-flavored vinegars, dipping oils, fresh-brewed coffee, serving pieces, and much more.

Hattich Ranch and Farm, 1236 Hagen Rd., Napa, CA 94558; (707) 294-4490; www.hattichranchandfarm.com, and on Facebook. With prior arrangement, Bob Hattich enjoys showing visitors what his family grows on the farm and how it's accomplished. Nearly 3 acres are devoted to berries alone: blackberries, boysenberries, blueberries, and raspberries. From late spring to early fall, the berries are sold at the ranch and at the local farmers' markets. (Hattich Ranch berries can be found in some of the jellies, jams, and preserves made by **Hurley Farms**—see listing in Made or Grown Here). Hattich Ranch also sells the berry plants, bare root or potted, in winter and early spring. Bob has been raising heirloom tomatoes since 2005, and he sells the juicy fruits to many local restaurants, too. The tomato plants are sold in early spring for home gardeners, along with pepper plants—hot or mild, there's something for every taste and recipe. No synthetic fertilizers are used at Hattich Ranch, and the farmers rely on the local wildlife (owls, bats, and bluebirds) to keep pests under control. Part of this property was once a large dairy operation between the 1930s and the 1960s. In the 1970s, the Hattich family bought a portion of the parcel, and two of the dairy barns are still there today. Please call ahead for a tour with Bob.

Hoffman Farm, 2125 Silverado Trail, Napa, CA 94558; (707) 226-8938. Usually open every day between August and November (look for the sign by the side of the road), this 23-acre family farm is famous for its walnuts, persimmons, Bartlett pears, and other fruit. The Hoffman family has kept the farm planted in fruit and nut trees since they first purchased it in 1949, and today it is one of the last large parcels of land in Napa Valley without wine grapes (which are much more profitable) growing at least somewhere on the property. When the Hoffmans bought the place, the orchard was mostly plum trees, for processing into prunes. As the market for prunes began to shrink, the family branched out into Hartley English walnut trees, and apple, pear, and peach trees. The fruits and nuts are no longer chemically treated for insects and disease, and so are left "organic"—blemishes and all. The hundreds of u-pick customers who stop by every fall don't care about a tiny worm here or a small bruise there. Fresh-off-the-tree fruits and nuts are still superior to produce trucked in from someplace else.

Marshall's Farm Natural Honey, 159 Lombardi Rd., American Canyon, CA 94503; (707) 556-8088 or (800) 624-4637; www.marshalls honey.com. Honey-and-food pairings—who knew? It's one of the options available at this entertaining diversion well south of the city of Napa, bordering on the town of American Canyon, a bedroom community known primarily for its devotion to chain stores of all kinds (looking for a Walmart?—it's here) and the roadside blight that goes with it. It seems an odd spot for a honey "farm" to operate, just a short distance off the busy, four-lane Highway 29, but there is much to see here in the pursuit of honey wisdom. The beekeeper, Spencer Marshall, sources honey from many microclimates within the San Francisco Bay Area. Honey can vary greatly in taste, texture, and color between one place and another, even if it's only a few miles. Drop in Monday through Friday between 10 a.m. and 5 p.m. and take a look around, or arrange for a 2-hour weekend tour for individuals or groups, or a school tour on Wednesdays and Thursdays—all by appointment only, and reasonably priced. The tours include a 20-minute film about bees and beekeeping, followed by a honey-and-food pairing and the tasting of as many as 25 honey varieties. A beehive is then opened for exploration, followed by a honey extracting demonstration and bottling of the thick, golden nectar. The beekeeping workshop requires you to get adequately suited up to work on the active beehives to learn about beekeeping and "hive to table" harvesting. If all you want is the honey, Marshalls' products are usually available for sale at Whole Foods Market in Napa, Ranch Market Too in Yountville, the Oakville Grocery in Oakville, and the Culinary Institute of America in St. Helena.

Napa Farmer's Market, parking lot at the Oxbow Public Market, 610 First St., Napa, CA 94559; (707) 252-7142; www.napafarmers market.com. From May through October, on Tuesday and Saturday mornings between 8:30 a.m. and noon, the parking lot at the former Copia center is taken over by area farmers and artisan food purveyors selling their vegetables, olive oils, honey, organic eggs, flowers, berries of all types, and organic mushrooms. For sustenance while you fondle fresh produce, count on hot tamales, cookies, vegan pastries, custom drip coffee, biscotti, and Afghan and Brazilian specialty items. Need your knives sharpened? One vendor provides that service. Another sells vermicompost and worm tea, a natural fertilizer and fungicide made from tap water, worm castings, and molasses (and cleverly packaged in a wine bottle) for enriching the soil in your home garden.

Omi's Farm, 4185 Silverado Trail, Napa, CA 94558; (707) 224-0954; www.silveradotrail.com and on Facebook. Pet-friendly and family oriented, Omi's Farm is open daily by appointment, so please call ahead before dropping by to purchase fresh eggs or spring rhubarb. The farm grows seasonal vegetables, fruits, and nuts, along with wine grapes from a small Cabernet Sauvignon vineyard (sorry, no wine tasting). Say hello to the animals, too: sheep, rabbits, chickens, turkeys, and Australian cattle dogs.

Made or Grown Here

Annie the Baker Cookies, (707) 812-5566; www.anniethebaker .com. Puffy cookies that stay light and moist—that's Annie's method of baking, and her motto is "for those who love cookie dough more than the cookie." Annie switched careers a few years back, from working in a bank in Chicago to enrolling in the pastry arts program at the Culinary Institute of America, up the highway in St. Helena. She was pastry chef at Mustards Grill when she decided to create a line of her own cookies. After much experimentation, Annie came up with the correct ratio of ingredients so that the puffy cookies are always perfect. All made from scratch, the cookies are available online or at such Napa Valley stores as Ritual Coffee Roasters and Tillerman Tea (in the Oxbow Public Market), Yountville Deli, NapaStyle, Sunshine Foods, Dean & DeLuca, and Cal Mart. The flavors include tuxedo macadamia, doodle snicker, toffee milk-chocolate chip, and double chocolate chip. Annie also sells her cookies at the seasonal farmers' markets in Napa Valley.

Atlas Peak Olive Oil, (707) 246-8011; www.atlaspeakoliveoil .com. Since 1882, the Hammond family has been harvesting olives on 240 acres approximately 2,000 feet above the Napa Valley floor. Hundreds of olive trees are grown on the ranch, including Spanish and Italian varieties, in an environment that's perfect for nurturing olives. It's not possible to visit the ranch, but owner Cathy Hammond sells her bottled olive oils and jars of whole olives at the seasonal farmers' markets in Napa Valley, or she can deliver them to you locally. Out of the area? Order the products from her website.

BOCA Farm, P.O. Box 5449, Napa, CA 94581; (707) 266-4926; www.bocafarm.org. BOCA's output is nearly all heirloom, organic produce grown for several high-end Napa Valley restaurants, from winter squash to carrots to herbs. Located on approximately 7 acres, the farm operates a community garden (call or visit the website to learn more) and a kids' garden, too. Produce is not for sale here, but visitors are usually welcome to look around if they call ahead first. Ask for Lizzie Moore for directions and more information.

Hudson Ranch, 5398 Carneros/Sonoma Hwy. (Hwy. 12/121), Napa, CA 94559; (707) 255-1455; www.hudsonranch.com. Raising animals without hormones or antibiotics and growing produce in the most sustainable way possible, Hudson Ranch also operates a community-supported agriculture (CSA) program. It's one of the first CSAs in Napa Valley, where the idea caught on much later than in other parts of the region. Chickens are available for purchase year-round, ranging in size from 3 to 4 pounds, along with fresh eggs. Hudson Ranch also raises pigs, turkeys, and guinea hens for meat, and sells many of their fruits and vegetables at the produce store at the Oxbow Public Market in downtown Napa. (Like many local farms, Hudson sells much of its produce directly to area restaurants.) The ranch has some vineyards, sure, but also an abundance of olive trees. The olives are picked in November and pressed locally into oil sold under the Titi's Extra Virgin Olive Oil label. You're welcome to visit the sprawling ranch if you call ahead, and Spencer Reid, the sales and project manager, can show you around. Produce is not sold on-site, but Spencer can sign you up for the CSA program, available in a small "share" or a medium, depending on your needs. In addition to lots of spring, summer, and fall vegetables and

fruits, your CSA package options might be eggs, chickens, or a guinea hen or two. Ask Spencer for the details, or check the ranch's website for the latest.

Hurley Farms, 2083 Silverado Trail, Napa, CA 94558; (707) 257-3683; www.hurleyfarms.com. As a small commercial operation making jams and jellies, fruit- and wine-flavored vinegars, mustards, and much more, Hurley Farms is not set up to receive visitors at this time. They grow much of the fruit used in their products on 4 acres along the Silverado Trail, and process and cook small, handmade batches of the food on-site. The farm also uses fruit from other local ranches when necessary. The easiest way to purchase Hurley's products is through the website, but you might also spot a few of their jams and jellies in local stores.

La Saison, (707) 637-3722; www.lasaison.net. Husband-and-wife chefs Jonathan Niksa and Natalie Niksa are Culinary Institute of America graduates with their own catering business and a line of delicious munchies sold under the La Saison brand. Most commonly found in Napa Valley stores is the date wheel, a rich mixture of Medjool dates and toasted pecans that can be thinly sliced for serving with cheese and red wine. It's usually available in a full or half wheel, and can be purchased on the chefs' website or at such Napa Valley retail outlets as Dean & DeLuca, Whole Foods Market, Vallerga's Market, the Cheese Merchant in the Oxbow Public Market, and several others. You might also find La Saison products at the farmers' markets in Napa and St. Helena.

Napa Cookie Company, 101 S. Coombs St., Napa, CA 94559; (707) 252-7265; www.napacookieco.com. White or red? Wine Snaps, that is. Found in some winery gift shops, the two different cookies are formulated to go with either white wine or red wine. Created by a longtime caterer, Melissa Teaff, and made in her Napa kitchen, Wine Snaps are sweet and salty shortbread biscuits that pair well with many toppings to heighten the enjoyment of wine. Look for Wine Snaps for sale on the website, and at local outlets such as Vallerga's Market, Back Room Wines, Cal Mart, and the Oakville Grocery.

Napa Farmhouse 1885, www.napafarmhouse 1885.com. Proprietor Diane Padoven whips up chutneys and marmalades made from the fruit grown in her Napa Valley yard—figs, limes, Meyer lemons, mandarin oranges, persimmons, and pears. She also creates seasoning blends, such as *herbes de Provence* and her Farmhouse organic rub. Try Diane's cocktail biscuits, too (her popular dog biscuits, retooled for humans), three different kinds of granola, and many nonfood items, as well. Diane believes in reusing whatever she can, so her containers feature labels made from recycled materials, and are usually topped with pages ripped from magazines. Look for Napa Farmhouse 1885 products in local shops, or order online.

Tulocay & Company, 388 Devlin Rd., Napa, CA 94558; (888) NAPA-VLY; www.tulocayandco.com, and www.madeinnapavalley .com. You'll see the "Made in Napa Valley" label on many bottled and jarred premium food products in retail locations around the area and throughout the nation, and this is where they are made. The facility is south of the city of Napa, in the light manufacturing area near the Napa County Airport, just off Highway 29. Founded almost 30 years ago, Tulocay began with a single product: etched olive oil decanters sold to wineries, hotels, and private-label customers. That led to food production, including an assortment of olive oils and flavored vinegars for retailers such as Crate & Barrel, Pier 1, and Dean & DeLuca. The Made in Napa Valley brand of high-end gourmet food products includes dipping oils, marinades, simmer sauces, rubs, and tapenades. Though the ingredients are not sourced locally, the products are inspired by wine-country cooking methods and flavors. Tulocay now produces five house brands, including the Vineyard Pantry and Tyler Florence Kitchen Essentials lines. The facility's retail shop stocks all the products that are manufactured on-site, and it's open Mon through Fri from 11:30 a.m. to 2:30 p.m. (come on "Foodie Fridays" and receive a 25 percent discount). An impressive on-site demonstration kitchen, operating as the Made in Napa Valley Culinary Centre, can accommodate up to 30 students. Watch the websites for the latest about cooking classes that are open to the public.

Wine Forest Wild Foods, 6493 Dry Creek Rd., Napa, CA 94558; (707) 944-8604; www.wineforest.com. Experienced foragers are aware that Napa Valley can yield amazing natural treasures, such as an abundance of chanterelle mushrooms at a certain time of year, along with wild fennel, English walnuts, pine nuts, and a few other tasty bits that can be used in gourmet meal preparation. Founded

Oxbow Public Market:
A One-Stop Shopping Experience

Since 2007, the Oxbow Public Market has steadily gained traction to become one of the many must-see features in the revitalized city of Napa. The lineup of eateries and food vendors has morphed somewhat since the Market first opened, but in spring 2011 it was fully occupied and launched a new restaurant, too, called Kitchen Door.

The Market is loosely modeled on the Ferry Plaza Marketplace in San Francisco (and conceived by the same team), and it's huge, too: 40,000 square feet.

I've included individual listings for many of the stores and food purveyors at Oxbow in this chapter, but there are several others worth noting:

Heritage Culinary Artifacts— Expect objects of art with a cooking or food connection, much of it whimsical. Select from copper pots, vintage salt-and-pepper shakers, and other antiques and curiosities.

Five Dot Ranch—A family operation, the beef raised by these ranchers comes from nine counties in northern California, including Napa Valley. The meat is all natural, and hormone- and antibiotic-free.

Hog Island Oyster Company and Kanaloa Seafood—The freshest bounty from the ocean can be found at these separate shops. Hog Island raises its oysters approximately straight west of Napa, in Tomales Bay, along the Pacific. The company also grows Manila clams and mussels. Their bar at Oxbow is a great place to grab a dozen ultrafresh oysters and kick back for happy hour from 5 to 7 p.m. on Tues and Wed. Also select from grilled oysters, salads, and stews and chowders.

Kanaloa is a big company that supplies sustainably raised fish primarily from the Pacific Ocean, covering a territory from Alaska to New Zealand. At the Oxbow outpost, Kanaloa usually has a full range of seafood to pick from, including sushi-grade ahi and mahi-mahi from Hawaii, ceviche, and crab cakes.

Oxbow Cheese Merchant and Oxbow Wine Merchant—More than 600 cheeses are featured at this store, waiting to be expertly matched with local and regional wines. Pull up a chair and prepare to learn the best ways to marry cheese with wine.

Oxbow Public Market

610 First St.
Napa, CA 94559
(707) 226-6529
www.oxbowpublicmarket.com

by master forager Connie Green, Wine Forest Wild Foods sources some of its inventory in Napa Valley, primarily the chanterelles. Connie has been supplying area chefs with fresh and dried mushrooms and other edible wild foods for many years. She says she is often asked if her wild chanterelles are organic—no, she explains, they're wild, so they are even better than organic (duh). Wine Forest Wild Foods is primarily a wholesaler to fine dining establishments in Napa Valley, San Francisco, and beyond. No tours are available, but you are welcome to navigate through the website to order mushrooms, pickled sea beans, truffle oils, wild juniper berries, and other culinary delicacies. If you're seeking a specific ingredient not offered on the website, call Kim Daniels at the number listed to discuss your options.

Food & Wine Pairings/ Landmark Wineries

Artesa Winery, 1345 Henry Rd., Napa, CA 94559; (707) 224-1668; www.artesawinery.com. It's safe to say that the view from this winery's terrace is one of the most impressive in all of Napa Valley, and the off-the-beaten-track drive in the Carneros district is worth it. At the higher elevation where the winery stands, you'll marvel at the 360-degree vista that extends even to the skyline of San Francisco on clear days, a distance of approximately 35 miles. Designed to blend into the landscape, the visitor center greets you with fountains and sculptures. Artesa is Spanish-owned (by Cordorniu, one of the world's largest producers of sparkling wine, called Cava in Spain) and it bottles some Cava here, but also still wines such as Pinot Noir, Merlot, Tempranillo, Cabernet Sauvignon, and Chardonnay. There are essentially three options for pairing the wines with food, and reservations are strongly recommended, as these tastings take place just once daily or on weekends only and are limited to a small number of people. With the "Vino con Queso," artisanal cheeses are matched with Artesa's limited-release and reserve wines in a private setting at the winery ($45 per person). Now for the good part: the "Chocolate Indulgence," where your guide pairs Artesa's Cabernet Sauvignon and sparkling wines with hand-picked chocolates and truffles created by Anette's Chocolates in Napa ($45 per person). For a larger fee ($75), a larger amount of food is prepared by the winery's resident chef, using local and organic ingredients, for pairing with Artesa's limited-release and small-production single-vineyard wines. The winery is open daily from 10 a.m. to 5 p.m.

Back Room Wines, First and Main streets, Napa, CA 94559; (707) 226-1378 or (877) 322-2576; www.backroomwines.com. When you don't know what wine to buy to go with a particular meal, Back Room Wines has the answer. This wine shop stocks small-production bottles from Napa Valley and other regions of California, many of them not easy to find elsewhere. Owner Dan Dawson is a guru at matching wines to specific foods, a skill he honed as sommelier at the French Laundry for many years, and a stint teaching wine education at Napa Valley College. Dan is a champion of wine-and-food pairings at his store, offering an assortment of cheese plates, along with anchovy-stuffed green olives and a mild chorizo sausage. The shop recently added monthly "Cheese Meets Wine" classes with cheese expert and author Janet Fletcher. The 90-minute sessions in the early evening ($55 per person) are designed to introduce students to six unusual cheeses that pair well with the four wines to be featured (example: sheep's milk cheese from Spain washed down with a nicely aged Napa Valley Cabernet Sauvignon). Reservations are required, as this has become a hot ticket with locals.

Darioush, 4240 Silverado Trail, Napa, CA 94558; (707) 257-2345; www.darioush.com. Driving up to this winery gets your attention. The building is modeled after the ancient capital of Persia, and 16 large columns, or "stone trees," lead you into the tasting room. The winery bottles a signature Cabernet Sauvignon, as well as Shiraz, Merlot, and Pinot Noir. Their "Duel" label is a blend of Cabernet Sauvignon and Shiraz. Though Darioush's production is primarily in reds, they also bottle two whites: Chardonnay and Viognier. Two options for food-and-wine pairing take place at Darioush. Offered daily at 2 p.m. is the "Fine Wines, Artisan Cheeses" experience for $50 per person. You receive a 90-minute private tour and a sit-down tasting of cheeses made by Cowgirl Creamery in neighboring Marin County (among others), matched with Darioush's special limited-release and library wines, which can't be tasted anywhere else. For an even grander time, pop for the "Quintessential" experience, two hours of sampling caviar with sparkling wine, followed by tasting other wines in the owner's private cellar. Each wine is paired with an amuse-bouche ("mouth amuser") created by Chef Ken Frank of La Toque restaurant in Napa. This type of exclusive tasting doesn't come cheap ($300 per person), and it's limited to a small group. Reservations must be made in advance for both of these food-and-wine pairings. The winery is open daily from 10:30 a.m. to 5 p.m.

Domaine Carneros, 1240 Duhig Rd., Napa, CA 94559; (800) 716-2788, or (707) 257-0101 to make reservations; www.domaine carneros.com. Perched grandly on a hillside overlooking the Carneros Highway, the structure is modeled after a country estate in France's Champagne district owned by the Taittinger family, the founders of this winery. It also has one of the most accessible food-and-wine pairings you'll find in Napa Valley, with several goodies to choose from. With no advance reservations necessary, you can enjoy table service between 10 a.m. and 5:45 p.m., either in the salon or on the terrace (and if the weather is fine, the terrace is where you really want to be). Domaine Carneros makes sparkling wine, Pinot Noir, Merlot, and Chardonnay. The wine tastings are available by the glass, by the bottle, or in "flights," generally meaning tastes of several vintages of the same varietal, or a comparison of different varietals. If you choose to try the bubbly, the sparkling-wine cheese plate is an appropriate accompaniment of three artisanal cheeses, two made nearby and one from France. Going directly to red wine? That cheese plate comes with Gorgonzola and two others (each cheese plate is $15). Take your food tasting to the next level by adding smoked salmon or caviar ($15 to $85, depending on your choice). You can also keep it light with a pastry plate for $7.50. In-depth, 60-minute tours are also possible, from $85 to $250 (and include some great parting gifts). During the busiest season (summer), it's smart to make reservations for the in-depth tours to avoid disappointment.

Etude Winery, 1250 Cuttings Wharf Rd., Napa, CA 94559; (707) 257-5300 or (877) 586-9361; www.etudewines.com. Etude produces high-end Cabernet Sauvignon and Pinot Noir in the Carneros grape-growing district, and they like to show them off with targeted food-and-wine pairings three times daily on Fri and Sat. For $35 per person (reservations required), you can savor tastes of six Etude wines expertly teamed with a bit of smoked rabbit in puff pastry, or eggplant and goat cheese, or a braised short rib terrine, and ending with a Moroccan-spiced chocolate truffle. In addition to red wine, Etude bottles some whites such as Chardonnay and Pinot Gris, as well as a rosé and a pricey, exquisite brandy. The winery practices sustainable farming techniques in its vineyards, including the use of a falconer and a team of falcons to keep the low-yielding heirloom Pinot Noir berries from being gobbled by hungry starlings at harvest time. The winery is open daily from 10 a.m. to 4:30 p.m. for tasting without an appointment.

Hess Collection, 4411 Redwood Rd., Napa, CA 94558; (707) 255-1144 or (877) 707-HESS; www.hesscollection.com. After you complete the $15 food-and-wine tasting in the winery's garden courtyard (spring through fall, weather permitting), you'll want to stick around to take a self-tour of the phenomenal modern art collection assembled by Donald Hess, a Swiss-born business tycoon (hence the "collection" in the name). Donald says he's not swayed by art "trends"— he just collects pieces that touch him deeply. The artists who touch him deeply include such notable names as Robert Motherwell, Francis Bacon, and Franz Gertsch. Certainly, many of these pieces will make you stop and ponder how they came to be created—as I have pondered myself. Now about the food. The winery's executive chef, Chad Hendrickson, is kept busy selecting just the right cheeses and whipping up the best bits of culinary excellence for pairing with Hess wines. There are several tasting options to choose from. The "Tour of the Palate" takes place on Thurs, Fri, and Sat, beginning with a guided stroll through the art museum and followed by the wine-and-food combinations ($50 per person). A wine-and-cheese pairing along with the art museum tour is less expensive ($35 per person). A wine-only tutorial (monthly in summer only) goes extensively into the science of winemaking, from the growing of the grapes to the fermentation process ($30). All of these tasting experiences require advance reservations. Hess Collection is not hard to find, but it is a 10- to 15-minute drive from the Trancas Street/Redwood Road exit off

Highway 29. The winery and the art museum are open daily from 10 a.m. to 5:30 p.m.

Robert Sinskey Vineyards, 6320 Silverado Trail, Napa, CA 94558; (707) 944-9090 or (800) 869-2030; www.robertsinskey.com. RSV, as they refer to their winery, believes food and wine are inseparable. So their "Farm to Table" tour begins with a glass of wine, a small taste of exceptional food, and then a stroll through the winery's gardens. That's followed by more small bites, tartlets, and special treats created by RSV's kitchen to accompany the various wines being tasted. At $60 per person, the tour is by appointment only and limited to 8 or fewer participants. RSV's vineyards are 100 percent certified organic and biodynamic. The physical address for RSV is Napa, but it's closer to Yountville, east of the town near the intersection of Silverado Trail and the Yountville Cross Road. Open daily from 10 a.m. to 4:30 p.m.

Signorello Vineyards, 4500 Silverado Trail, Napa, CA 94559; (707) 255-5990; www.signorellovineyards.com. You may come for the food and wine, but you will linger here on the patio for the view of Napa Valley over the infinity edge pool (sorry, no swimming allowed). Signorello's culinary treats lean toward Italian influences, particularly the popular pizza-and-wine pairing for $45 per person (weekends from Apr through Oct, by appointment). The *margherita* pizzas big enough for two are baked in an outdoor wood-burning oven and paired with five tastes of Signorello's robust reds, such as Cabernet Sauvignon, Syrah, Pinot Noir, and Zinfandel. The winery also produces Chardonnay and Seta, a blend of Sauvignon Blanc and Semillon. A more extensive and private food-and-wine pairing and tour for $85 per person takes place twice daily (by reservation only). During the 90-minute tour you'll savor Signorello's Bordeaux-style Cabernet Sauvignon served with Kurobuta pork tenderloin and butternut squash, Dungeness crab and herbed gnocchi teamed with Chardonnay, pan-seared rabbit tenderloin with Zinfandel, and other lip-smacking combinations. For a special occasion, book the "Picnic for Two" experience ($150), which includes a full lunch of sandwiches, salads, dessert, and a bottle of wine—enjoyed in a secluded picnic area. The winery is open daily from 10 a.m. to 5 p.m.

Silverado Vineyards, 6121 Silverado Trail, Napa, CA 94558; (707) 257-1770; www.silveradovineyards.com. Walt Disney's daughter, Diane Disney Miller, has owned this winery for decades along with her husband, Ron Miller. They don't try to hide this fact, as you will see from the Disney artwork and history exhibit, nor do they try to capitalize on it. Silverado produces reds and whites, including a blend of Cabernet Sauvignon and Sangiovese called Fantasia (there's that family pride again). Sign up for the $35 per person wine-and-cheese pairing, or enhance your Silverado experience with a $75 private tour of the winery's Saddle Block vineyard, with seasonal bites of food (such as nuts, deviled eggs, and sliced beef) matched to the wine grown from the vines right there in front of you. The library tasting option pairs older vintages of Silverado's Cabernet Sauvignon with, perhaps, fresh Hog Island oysters from the not-so-far-away Pacific Ocean. All of these food-and-wine options require advance reservations. The winery is open daily from 10 a.m. to 4:30 p.m. for wine tasting only without an appointment.

Trefethen Vineyards, 1160 Oak Knoll Ave., Napa, CA 94558; (866) 895-7696; www.trefethen.com. The historic 3-story, gravity-flow winery building is one of the attractions at Trefethen. A Scottish sea captain, Hamden McIntyre, constructed the redwood winery, along with a few others in Napa Valley, including what is now the Culinary Institute of America in St. Helena. Built in 1886, the structure at Trefethen was restored a century later and is still used for wine storage and to house the tasting room and wine library. It's also a designated National Historic Landmark. History aside, the winery hosts a $100-per-person food-and-wine pairing called "Twilight at Trefethen," a 2-hour experience on Friday evening after the winery closes to the public that includes a tour along with cheese and charcuterie munchies. Then you sip small-lot vintages pulled straight from the winery's cellar and get an exclusive tasting of an aging Cabernet Sauvignon directly from the barrel. Reservations are required for this tasting. In addition to Cabernet Sauvignon, Trefethen bottles Merlot, Chardonnay, a dry Riesling, Pinot Noir, Cabernet Franc, and Viognier. Open from 10 a.m. to 4:30 p.m. daily.

Wineries of Napa Valley, 1285 Napa Town Center, Napa, CA 94559; (800) 328-7815 or (707) 254-9450; www.napavintages .com. Every few days, this wine bar (a "collective" representing several labels) in downtown Napa conducts a food-and-wine pairing from 4 to 6 p.m. for $10. One evening it's a seasonal bruschetta appetizer and a choice of five Napa boutique wines, and another night it could be a tri-tip steak appetizer, a pulled pork appetizer, grilled sausage, or cheese and olives paired with craft beers or the Napa wines. For chocolate enthusiasts, there's also a "Chocolate Decadence" tasting, when the sweets are matched with wine or stout beer. This wine bar spotlights smaller wineries, such as **Goosecross Cellars** (see the Yountville chapter), Destino Wines, Nord Estate Wines, Girard Winery, Burgess Cellars, and Lake County's Fore Family Vineyards.

Brewpubs & Microbreweries

Downtown Joe's Brewhouse, 902 Main St., Napa, CA 94559; (707) 258-2337; www.downtownjoes.com. You can spot Downtown Joe's by its bright teal exterior and color-matched tents over the riverside patio area. Housed in the Oberon building, which dates to 1894, the brewery got its start in 1988. A few years later, new owners stepped in and it became Downtown Joe's. Several brews are made here, with catchy names like Tail Waggin' Amber Ale, Catherine The Great Imperial Stout, and Golden Thistle Very Bitter Ale. Owner

Joe Peatman says that some of his brewery's beer is "very British" and some is "West Coast" style. The menu is heavy with traditional pub-type favorites, but with creative California twists. Whenever possible, Joe's sources sustainably harvested and organic ingredients, including the meat, poultry, and seafood. Start with sushi-grade ahi rolled in sunflower seeds on fried wontons, or prawns fried in the brewery's own wheat-beer batter. Main courses include bangers and mash, fish-and-chips, pork sliders, a *margherita* pizza, burgers, steaks, salads, cioppino, a pub steak sandwich, and so on. Whatever you order, it will wash down well with the suds.

Napa Smith Brewery, 1 Executive Way, Napa, CA 94559; (707) 255-2912; www.napasmithbrewery.com. For some time, the brewery has been giving tours and tastings only by prior appointment, but it's gearing up to accommodate drop-in visitors (it's still a good idea to call first before showing up). The tour and tasting of its beers is $10 per person, which includes a logo glass and some small bites of food. The brewery's Amber Ale, Pale Ale, and Lost Dog Red Ale all received gold medals recently at the California State Fair. Their organic IPA and Lost Dog Red Ale are probably the most widely distributed, and one or more of the brews can be found on the beer lists at many Napa Valley restaurants. If you like what you taste, pick up a four-pack of Napa Smith's ales at one of the area grocery stores such as Vallerga's Market, at Napa's JV Wine & Spirits wine store, and at Sunshine Foods in St. Helena and Cal Mart in Calistoga.

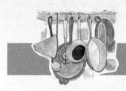

Cedar Gables Inn, 486 Coombs St., Napa, CA 94559; (707) 224-7969; www.cedargablesinn.com. Ken and Susie Pope, longtime owners of this bed-and-breakfast, emphasize fun in the food-and-wine instruction they offer. For more than 5 years they've attracted chefs from Napa Valley and beyond—such as Greg Cole, Bob Hurley, Ken Frank, and Joanne Weir—to lead the classes. The Popes' fabulous kitchen is tricked out for any type of culinary adventure, and the students sit down in style to enjoy their meal following the 4-hour preparation. The wine pairings are usually hosted by such exclusive wineries as Grgich Hills, Hagafen, and Porter Family Vineyards. Limited to 12 students (at $150 per person), the classes begin at 4 p.m. on a Sat and wrap up around 8 p.m.—dinnertime! A complimentary apron and the recipes are included in the tariff. Being an overnight guest at the inn is not a requirement to attend a class, but considering all the wine that is poured before and during the meal, you may want a designated driver or a taxi to get you safely back home or to your hotel. See Susie Pope's recipe for **French Toast Soufflé** on p. 225.

Cooking With Julie, P.O. Box 5412, Napa, CA 94581; (707) 227-5036; www.cookingwithjulie.com. It's possible to walk through the Oxbow Public Market on your own (perhaps aimlessly), but with Julie Logue-Riordan as your guide it becomes a learning experience, with opportunities to chat in-depth with the food purveyors. A Napa Valley resident, Julie is a certified culinary professional who offers several types of classes and tours for all skill levels. The intensive stroll through Oxbow (and the Napa Farmers' Market taking place outside) is how she sources many of the ingredients for the lunch you will prepare later in her class. Julie's Oxbow tour begins at 9 a.m. on Tues and Fri, wrapping up around 4 p.m., after she takes you to a winery for a private tasting, followed by the hands-on cooking. Tuck a linen napkin under your chin and you're ready to devour the delicious 3-course meal plated up on fine china in an elegant setting. Julie offers a similar tour that includes selecting produce directly from local farmers at the seasonal St. Helena Farmers' Market. If you seek a more extensive culinary adventure, she also schedules private classes lasting up to five days. Visit her website to learn the latest.

Fatted Calf Charcuterie, 644-C First St., Napa, CA 94559 (near the Oxbow Public Market); (707) 256-3684; www.fattedcalf.com. Meat lovers, rejoice! Every couple of Saturdays year-round, usually from 11 a.m. to 3 p.m., Fatted Calf conducts a class that demystifies the meat curing process. The current class lineup includes instruction in whole hog butchery, pâtés and terrines, *salumi,* duck, and a beginner's course in making sausage. Besides what you learn from the experts, you'll receive lunch and samples of the meats you helped prepare. These popular classes, at $150 per person, fill up early, so check the website frequently or call Fatted Calf directly to get your name on the list for the next available class.

Gourmet Walks

Starting at the Oxbow Public Market, these 3-hour walking tours end on the opposite bank of the Napa River at the Napa Mill complex. On a flat, easily paced 1-mile route you will learn about downtown Napa's history, art, and culinary scene from a local resident who acts as your guide. The basic tour is $68 per person. For an extra charge, reserve the chocolate truffle-making class or other themed cooking class after the walk. Even a 2-hour wine-blending class can be arranged. The walks take place on Fri and Sun beginning at 10:30 a.m. For more information: (415) 312-1119 or (855) 503-0697; www.gourmetwalks.com.

Hugh Carpenter's Cooking Schools & Camp Napa Culinary, 3960 Hagen Rd., Napa, CA 94558; (707) 252-9773 or (888) 999-4844; www.hughcarpenter.com. For more than 3 decades, professional chef and cookbook author Hugh Carpenter has been conducting cooking classes. Three or four times a year, in summer and fall, he leads a culinary camp in Napa Valley that lasts approximately 6 days. Hugh takes you on tours of boutique wineries and into exclusive kitchens where you will learn how to pair the food you make with dozens of California wine varietals. Limited to 16 students, the class "graduates" with a special dinner in, perhaps, a winery's private dining room.

Napa Walking Tour, (707) 694-5097; or www.napawalkingtour .com. Local historian and actor George Webber adds a dash of humor and vintage costumes to his interesting 3-hour walking tours of downtown Napa's colorful history and its hodgepodge of architectural styles. The tours start at 9:30 a.m. at the Napa Mill complex and include a wine tasting and entertaining lecture from "Professor Vine" (that's George in character), as well as a beer tasting at Downtown Joe's on Main Street. Priced at $35 per person, it's inexpensive and fun, too. Reservations are required.

Whole Foods Market Culinary Center, 3682 Bel Aire Plaza, Napa, CA 94558; (707) 224-6300; www.wholefoods.com. Culinary director Marina Kercher came on board in 2011 with fresh ideas for this Napa outpost of the nationwide chain, and has succeeded in signing up Napans in a variety of culinary classes. She has lined up guest chefs, cookbook signings, and many similar food-related events, while also offering inexpensive instruction ranging from filleting a fish to preparing vegan cuisine. The market's large demonstration kitchen has seating around the counter for small groups and two monitors overhead for larger classes (up to 22 students) to watch the action. Cooking classes for couples are offered at $160. Winemaker dinners are also part of the mix, at about $60 to $75 per person. Family dinner classes, with parents and children cooking together and sharing the finished meal, are among the possibilities, too. In summer, children as young as 4 can take part in a cooking "camp"—2-hour-long classes in which kids learn to make a simple dish.

Yountville

A small, rural town with a population of less than 3,000 hardly seems like the sort of place that would attract people from all over the world in search of an unforgettable meal. Yet Yountville is such a place.

Nearly all of the dining, shopping, and lodging in Yountville is concentrated along Washington Street, which is parallel to Highway 29. Because of the town's compact size, it's possible to park the car once when you arrive and wander with ease from one end of Washington Street to the other, stopping to peek into wine-tasting rooms, stores, and restaurant windows. During your stroll, take a short time-out in the tiny but meticulously clean Van de Leur Park, where you can read a bit of history of how Yountville came to be.

Mountain man George Yount, originally from North Carolina, headed west across the continent in the early 1800s with a group of rugged travelers like himself. At that time, Native Americans were the primary residents of northern California, so George is generally considered to be the first nonnative to put down roots in this region. By all accounts he was clever and enterprising. He planted wheat and potatoes, established a small vineyard, and built a flour mill and a sawmill. He also cranked out a huge quantity of shingles for the hacienda being constructed by Mexican commandant Mariano Vallejo (known later as General Vallejo). History states that for this achievement George received the nearly 12,000-acre Mexican land grant known as Rancho Caymus. In 1859, he sold a parcel of the land to found the small town of Sebastopol, which was already the name of a settlement to the west. A couple of years after George Yount died, the town was renamed Yountville in his honor. (George is buried in Pioneer Cemetery, at the north end of Yountville Park.)

Today, locals like to joke that Yountville should be renamed once again, to "Kellerville." That's because world-renowned chef Thomas Keller owns three restaurants and a bakery along Washington Street, and he is largely responsible for the town's current reputation as a culinary mecca. It all began with Keller's purchase of the French Laundry restaurant in 1994. Four years later he opened Bouchon, and several years after that came Ad Hoc—see the listings for all in this chapter. In the meantime, other chefs and hotel operators began opening restaurants and building or expanding luxury lodgings and spas, while the old stone winery that is now called V Marketplace filled up with chic shops. The curious and the hungry started coming by the thousands.

Yountville has learned to adapt to the hustle and bustle of visitors. Its popularity has been mostly good for the community, of course, even though traffic can be frustrating at times and the sidewalks crowded with shoppers and gawkers on weekends and for special events. Still, only a block or two off Washington Street the town's residents go on with their lives in pretty, well-tended neighborhoods.

In 2011, a total of six Michelin stars were bestowed upon restaurants in Yountville, the most per capita of anyplace in the world. In the culinary universe, receiving one, two, or three Michelin stars is generally considered the equivalent of winning one, two, or three Academy Awards. It's sort of a big deal.

Landmark Eateries

Ad Hoc, 6476 Washington St., Yountville, CA 94599; (707) 944-2487; www.adhocrestaurant.com; $$$$. In 2006, Chef Thomas Keller opened this restaurant to offer affordable, casual dining while he developed another restaurant concept for the site (for burgers and wine). Ad Hoc was supposed to be temporary, but it became so popular that Keller's other plans were abandoned for the time being. The fixed-price menu for dinner is currently $52 (suggested wine pairings at $39 are extra). On a recent evening the meal began with endive and watercress salad with toasted hazelnuts and Granny Smith apple vinaigrette. That was followed by buttermilk-fried chicken accompanied by baby artichoke, turnips, carrot and celery stew, and potatoes. The sweet finish was *tres leches* cake with strawberries. On another night, rack of pork or beef short ribs might have the starring role. Seating is mostly inside, but a small patio accommodates 12. Dinner is served starting at 5 p.m. Thurs through Mon; brunch is on Sun beginning at 10 a.m.

Bistro Jeanty, 6510 Washington St., Yountville, CA 94599; (707) 944-0103; www.bistrojeanty.com; $$. Billed as the only French-owned and -operated restaurant in Napa Valley, this bistro's food is also considered the most authentic, without actually having to go to France. Philippe Jeanty was raised in the Champagne region of France, a rural agricultural area where he learned to appreciate growing produce and raising animals for the family farm. He came to California in 1977 after receiving chef's training in his home-land, and went to work at the first restaurant at Domaine Chandon, which became famous for its fine French cuisine. In 1998, Philippe decided to open his own bistro to showcase his favorite foods from childhood. At Bistro Jeanty you can expect such French classics as cassoulet, steak tartare, coq au vin, sole meunière, quiche *aux poireaux,* filet au poivre, and *daube de boeuf.* Once on the short list to be named "Best New Restaurant in America" by the James Beard Foundation, Bistro Jeanty has also received Michelin recognition in the San Francisco edition of the guide. Open daily from 11:30 a.m. to 10:30 p.m.

Bottega, 6525 Washington St., Yountville, CA 94599; (707) 945-1050; www.botteganapavalley.com; $$$. Michael Chiarello is not shy in front of a camera. The chef who founded **Tra Vigne** in St.

Helena (see that chapter) gave up the daily kitchen grind for several years while he taped cooking shows for television (including an Emmy winner), wrote several cookbooks, and launched his NapaStyle retail enterprise. He's high-profile, but he's also the real deal: a hard-working chef who adores and creates innovative Italian cuisine. In 2009 he opened Bottega to get back to his love of cooking, and the crowds have beaten a path to his door. Many of the diners are star-struck, hoping to get an autographed cookbook or a quick snapshot with the chef. More times than not, he obliges. But what brings people back is the food, not the flash. Pasta has a large presence on the menu, but other interesting twists such as "polenta under glass" are also big hits (it's served in a glass jar, then topped with mushrooms and balsamic game sauce). Main courses are meaty, including confit of half duck, twice-cooked pork chop, short ribs, chicken, and crab and scallop entrees.

The restaurant is large (seating approximately 100 inside) and the interior is striking. The decor maintains much of the brick-and-beam charm of the original old winery building it occupies, yet is made softer and warmer with Italian chandeliers and rich fabrics. Lunch is available Tues through Sun from 11:30 a.m. to 2:30 p.m., and dinner is served until 9:30 p.m. (to 10 p.m. on weekends). Chef Chiarello's **NapaStyle** store is directly across from Bottega's entry.

Bouchon, 6534 Washington St., Yountville, CA 94599; (707) 944-8037; www.bouchonbistro.com; $$$. Bouchon was Thomas Keller's second venture into fine dining in Yountville, after his flagship French Laundry and before Ad Hoc. While the French Laundry may be too exclusive and pricey for many people, Bouchon is more accessible, less expensive, and doesn't require reservations exactly two months in advance. This is French bistro food "rooted in tradition," as Keller describes the menu, in the type of place that reminds the chef of his adventures traveling through France. Entrees can include pan-roasted trout with marinated grapes, sunchokes, fennel, marcona almonds, and *beurre noisette; croque madame* or steak frites; and roasted leg of lamb with turnips and Swiss chard. Even though this building was once believed to house a Wells Fargo office, today it's a little bit of Paris accented with a tin ceiling, Art Deco–style light fixtures, and mosaiclike tile floors. Bouchon opens daily at 11:30 a.m. and has always been known for staying open late—dinner is served until 12:30 a.m. Because of this, it draws local winery workers, along with chefs and staff from other restaurants long closed for the night. (There are two other Bouchon locations in the United States, in Las Vegas and Beverly Hills.)

The French Laundry, 6640 Washington St., Yountville, CA 94599; (707) 944-2380; www.frenchlaundry.com; $$$$. Thomas Keller's internationally acclaimed restaurant is the reason many people come to Yountville. Most don't have reservations, which can be challenging to arrange, nor the budget to enjoy a meal there. Some want only to look at the building (on the National Register of Historic Places), take a photograph, and gaze upon the 2 acres of beautifully sculpted gardens directly across the street, where much of the kitchen's produce is grown. Chef Keller took over the French Laundry in 1994 and quickly gained fame, attracting eager gourmets seeking one of its 64 seats. For many years, the restaurant has been regarded as the best in the nation, and some have gone so far as to call it the best in the world. Keller is the only chef in America with two Michelin three-star restaurants (the other is Per Se, in New York City). Even the French admire him, and that's saying something. In 2011, Keller was awarded France's highest decoration, the Legion d'Honneur, and named Chevalier for his efforts in promoting French cuisine in America (it's akin to being knighted in Britain). In the food field, he joins only two other Americans to receive that recognition: Julia Child and Alice Waters. Keller is a nice, humble fellow, and I've enjoyed one of his signature creations, cornets of salmon tartare, a couple of times at local events (they are a wee bit of heaven, I can assure you). Currently, the French Laundry's 9-course prix-fixe dinner or lunch is $270 per person (including service charge, although wine is extra). Some of Keller's famous and enduring dishes are pearl tapioca with oysters and caviar, hand-cut tagliatelle with Périgord truffles, butter-poached Maine lobster, Haas avocado salad with Persian lime sorbet—and so on. Lunch is Fri through Sun; dinner is nightly. Reservations must be made two months in advance.

Mustards Grill, 7399 St. Helena Hwy. (Hwy. 29), Napa, CA 94558; (707) 944-2424; www.mustardsgrill.com; $$. Wild mustard explodes into bright blossoms throughout Napa Valley in late winter and early spring. Those lovely yellow flowers were Chef Cindy Pawlcyn's inspiration for naming this restaurant, her first in Napa Valley. Open since 1983, Mustards is still a major attraction for visitors and locals, so count on a wait at peak times if you haven't made a reservation. Cindy likes to say that she's been serving "deluxe truck stop classics" for almost 30 years, and much of the menu is comfort food with a bit of an Asian twist. Cindy's Sonoma rabbit "au vin" is always on the menu, as are the half-pound hamburgers, pasta, calf's liver, three-cheese macaroni and cheese, corn sticks, and other longtime favorites. Cindy was one of the first chefs in Napa Valley to install an organic garden at a restaurant site to provide produce for meal preparation, so the two acres adjacent to Mustards are brimming year-round with seasonally fresh vegetables, fruits, and herbs. Diners are welcome to stroll through the gardens before or after their meal to develop an appreciation for how produce is grown. Mustards is only a short distance north of Yountville on Highway 29 (St. Helena Highway). Open daily at 11:30 a.m. (11 a.m. on Sat and Sun), and until 9 p.m. Mon through Thurs, and Sun (to 10 p.m. Fri and Sat).

Redd, 6480 Washington St., Yountville, CA 94599; (707) 944-2222; www.reddnapavalley.com; $$$. Richard Reddington cheffed in San Francisco, Europe, Beverly Hills, and at Napa Valley's Auberge du

Soleil before opening his namesake restaurant in Yountville in 2005. French-trained, Chef Reddington serves what he refers to as "Napa Valley contemporary cuisine." This might include sautéed skate with butternut squash, root vegetables, spinach, and pine-nut butter; or duck confit with lentils, *foie gras* meatballs, and crispy spaetzle; or California sea bass with potato puree, brussels sprouts, and bacon. There are also tasting menu options for lunch and dinner, and a bar menu offering fish tacos, prosciutto pizza, and pork and shrimp pot stickers. Alfresco patio dining, too. Open for lunch and dinner daily: lunch from 11:30 a.m. to 2:30 p.m., dinner from 5:30 to 9:30 p.m., and Sunday brunch from 11 a.m. to 2:30 p.m.

Foodie Faves

Brix, 7377 St. Helena Hwy. (Hwy. 29), Napa, CA 94558; (707) 944-2749; www.brix.com; $$$. The house favorite at Brix is the porcini-rubbed rib eye steak served with blue cheese and trumpet mushrooms. Too heavy? Go lighter with the charcoal-grilled, line-caught swordfish with brussels sprouts. Other options are lamb osso buco, braised beef bolognese, and grilled tenderloin. The focus at Brix is on cuisine reminiscent of northern Italy and southern France. (The bar menu offers a seasonal hamburger, laughing bird shrimp, and cast-iron mussels.) Brix is also a wine shop, with rows of small-production wines—roughly 800 bottles—and accoutrements for entertaining, such as table linens, glassware, and decanters. Set on

16 acres, the restaurant relies on its extensive fruit and vegetable gardens on the grounds. Crops are grown year-round to supply the salad greens, strawberries, beans, eggplants, tomatoes, apples, pears, squash, potatoes, herbs, and other produce used in the kitchen for meal preparation. Brix is slightly north of Yountville on Highway 29 (St. Helena Highway). The prevailing color scheme inside and out is a fresh golden yellow. Open for lunch daily from 11:30 a.m. to 3 p.m. (the bar menu is featured from 3 to 9 p.m.) and dinner is served daily from 5 to 9 p.m. Sunday brunch is from 10 a.m. to 2 p.m. See Brix's recipe for **Crispy Fried Green Beans with Hot Mustard Sauce** on p. 231.

Étoile at Domaine Chandon, 1 California Dr., Yountville, CA 94599; (888) 242-6366; www.chandon.com; $$$. Calling itself the only fine-dining restaurant within a winery in Napa Valley, Étoile serves French-inspired California cuisine. Venison, prime rib, lamb loin, and duck breast are on the menu, along with stinging-nettle risotto, lobster dumplings, spiced pork belly and smoked octopus, and calf's liver. Seared *foie gras* with a lentil ragout might get your meal off to a memorable start. Domaine Chandon is on the west side of Highway 29, reached at the south end of Yountville. Take California Drive under the highway, then a right turn at the sign for Domaine Chandon; the winery and restaurant are on the hillside. Open for lunch from 11:30 a.m. to 2:30 p.m. Thurs through Mon; dinner from 6 to 9 p.m. Thurs through Mon.

Hurley's, 6518 Washington St., Yountville, CA 94599; (707) 944-2345; www.hurleysrestaurant.com; $$. Where do the locals eat? It's a question often asked by visitors who arrive in Yountville seeking good food at good prices, and in good company. Chef Bob Hurley opened this restaurant in 2002, and because of its late-night dining option, many locals end up at Hurley's after the visitors have gone back to their hotels. On the menu are house-made gnocchi, squash ravioli, vegetable risotto, linguine with shrimp, ahi tuna, salmon, roasted chicken, wild Texas boar, and short ribs. Start with an onion tart, crab cakes, calamari, grilled mussels steamed with chorizo, or beef skewers. Hurley's offers a gluten-free menu, too—just ask. Every autumn Bob sets aside a week to serve wild game in intriguing ways: venison goulash, elk sirloin, pancetta-wrapped quail, grilled octopus, ostrich medallions, antelope short ribs, buffalo rib eye, and roasted pheasant. Wines by the glass are reasonable, starting at $7, with most in the $9 to $11 range. Hurley's opens at 11:30 a.m. daily and serves until midnight.

Pacific Blues Cafe, 6525 Washington St., Yountville, CA 94599; (707) 944-4455; www.pacificbluescafe.com; $$. Before Hurley's, before Redd, and long before Bottega, this place was dishing up tasty fare—what the owners call "maverick" American cuisine—for breakfast, lunch, and dinner. It may also have the best alfresco dining in town for people watching and scenery gazing. Housed in what was once the town's train depot, the restaurant makes generous use of train decor. The Pacific line ran through Yountville, and the music on the sound system is blues—this explains the name. The railroad theme doesn't end there. On the patio, you're likely to see the real Napa Valley Wine Train chugging by along Highway 29 as you tuck into fried chicken, grilled polenta, or blue-cheese sliders. End your meal snacking on Rice Krispie treats with caramel and hot-fudge dipping sauce. A wine bar has been added at the restaurant, also pouring a wide variety of beer on tap. Open daily from 8 a.m. to 9 p.m.

The Restaurant at Bardessono, 6526 Yount St., Yountville, CA 94599; (707) 204-6030; www.bardessono.com/restaurant_bar; $$$. Bardessono is a small, high-end resort and spa, and the greenest luxury hotel in America. In 2010, one year after opening, Bardessono received the highest level of official recognition possible for its sustainable and environmentally friendly design: LEED Platinum certification. At the time, it was one of only three hotels in the world to achieve that distinction. So when a hotel is green to the nth degree, how does that impact the menu? Like most restaurants in Napa Valley, Bardessono sources as many local organic, artisanal, and biodynamically grown ingredients as possible. Because of this, the breakfast, lunch, and dinner menus change every few days depending on the season and the availability of the freshest produce and meat. In addition to specific dinner entrees such as lamb, pork, chicken, duck, and seafood, a 6-course tasting menu can be ordered. The lounge also serves lunch daily, consisting of soups and salads, sandwiches, and shared cheese and charcuterie plates. Guests of the hotel can also dine poolside in summer and fall, in addition to ordering room service.

Tacos Garcia Truck, parking lot of Pancha's bar, 6764 Washington St., Yountville, CA 94599; (707) 337-9195 or (707) 980-4896. It's serendipitous to find a taco truck only two blocks from the world-famous French Laundry, parked next to the local dive bar. Yet Tacos Garcia cooks up satisfying, authentic, inexpensive Mexican food, and does it quickly and efficiently. Customers are local workers (you might get into lively conversations with school teachers and landscapers as you wait for your order), and more adventurous types who want to experience pork stomach and beef tongue for the first time. Basic tacos start at $1.50, and burritos at $5—the best bargains in town. The shrimp burrito has a touch of spicy heat, and is generously filled with shellfish. The truck opens its windows at 11 a.m. Mon through Sat, and closes at 8 p.m. There's no seating on-site, but the lovely Yountville Park is only a block away—at the intersection of Madison and Washington streets—with picnic tables and restrooms. Tacos Garcia operates a second truck in Napa at 2985 Jefferson St.

Bouchon Bakery, 6528 Washington St., Yountville, CA 94599; (707) 944-2253; www.bouchonbakery.com. There's a confection in the bakery case that looks like pure sunshine. Called *tarte au citron,* it's too beautiful to destroy by eating, so I choose an expendable, buttery croissant instead. As in most bakeries, Bouchon produces pastries, breads, and cookies, and offers sandwiches for sale, too, all at reasonable prices. If your sweet tooth is aching, grab a chocolate éclair or chocolate rum baba. Is it lunchtime? Dig into the mushroom French dip, or an egg-and-lox sandwich. Don't forget about dinner: ask for a few Dutch crunch rolls, hot cross buns, or palladin rolls to go. Before making your choices, take a moment to admire the delicate artistry of the *épi* baguette, patterned after a stalk of wheat. Tables are right outside, if you can't wait to devour the goodies. The bakery is one of Thomas Keller's sublime culinary achievements, and the breads made here are also served at his restaurants nearby. Open daily 7 a.m. to 7 p.m. (There are three more of Chef Keller's Bouchon bakeries in America: in New York City's Rockefeller Center and Times Warner Center, and in Las Vegas at the Venetian casino resort.)

Kollar Chocolates, 6525 Washington St., Yountville, CA 94599 (in the V Marketplace); (707) 738-6750; www.kollarchocolates.com. Chefs trained to prepare savory dishes sometimes harbor a dark secret: they'd rather be making chocolate. Chris Kollar worked in restaurant kitchens around Napa Valley for 10 years before taking the plunge into chocolate full time, and he opened this store in spring 2011 to showcase his chocolate-making talents—a fusion of European-style techniques and flavors with new-world twists. Chris sells small-batch, handmade signature creations such as a saffron poppy bar and a fennel-pollen truffle. Gelato, espresso, and chocolate shots are also on the menu. At press time, Chris planned to offer workshops and demonstrations in chocolate making on- and off-site. Check his website or follow him on Facebook for the latest news.

NapaStyle at V Marketplace, 6525 Washington St., Yountville, CA 94599; (707) 945-1229; www.napastyle.com. Maybe I don't get out enough, but there is more salt in this store than I've ever seen before, even at my nearby gourmet grocery. Colorful labels on 4.5-ounce tins declare the many different types: gray, Sicilian white, Peruvian pink, Hawaiian red, black, English flake, Chardonnay and oak smoked, roasted garlic, and more. Taking this condiment to the next level is the Himalayan salt slab carved from pure salt crystals found deep underground in the Himalayas. These can be heated for searing food at the table, or frozen to chill sushi or desserts. I'm only a few steps into the store and already my mind is reeling with the salty possibilities. Chef Michael Chiarello's lifestyle and kitchen store adjacent to his **Bottega** restaurant (see Landmark Eateries) is a must-see for any cooking enthusiast. The space isn't huge but it's well stocked with a wine department (*enoteca*), a fill-your-own-bottle olive-oil station, shelves of cookbooks (many written and signed by Chiarello), vintage flatware, elegant table settings, glassware, cookware, gotta-have-it furniture and decor, a tasting bar pouring several Chiarello Family Vineyards wines (three tastes for $15), and a panini cafe in the back. Pick up a NapaStyle catalog to see other food-preparation and dining items you never knew existed. Open 10 a.m. to 6 p.m. Sun through Wed, and 10 a.m. to 8 p.m. Thurs through Sat.

Ranch Market Too, 6498 Washington St., Yountville, CA 94599; (707) 944-2662; www.ranchmarketnapavalley.com. This family-owned market is one of the older businesses in modern Yountville, and almost everyone stops in for provisions or gifts during their stay in town. It's the combination of a good convenience store, a gift shop, and a wine shop. Of course, you can buy practical items like soap or dental floss, but it's also the quickest source for the Wine-opoly game (a clever retooling of Monopoly for wine geeks), gourmet treats, artisanal cheese, olive oils, and on-the-go cold drinks. The "Too" in the market's name refers to it being one of two locations; the other is in the city of Napa, at 4215 Solano Avenue. (Yountville Deli is at the north end of the store.) Open 6 a.m. to 10 p.m. every day.

Yountville Coffee Caboose, 6523 Washington St., Yountville, CA 94599; (707) 738-1153; www.yountvillecoffeecaboose.com. What you see is what you get: a small coffee shop in a renovated caboose, located up the ramp at the entrance to the Napa Valley Railway Inn (with deluxe rooms all in old rail cars). Order French-pressed joe or espresso, then relax on the deck overlooking V Marketplace and the activity on Washington Street. Sweet bakery treats are for sale, too. Open Mon to Fri from 7 a.m. to 5:30 p.m., weekends 8 a.m. to 5:30 p.m.

Yountville Deli, 6498 Washington St., Yountville, CA 94599; (707) 944-2002; www.yountvilledeli.com. A deli where you can call ahead to reserve a fresh salad—what a concept! Choose a Cobb, chef's, chicken Caesar, or Chinese chicken. It's the sandwiches that bring in the locals in a hurry, salivating for the generous deli meats on a choice of several breads, including fabulous rolls made just a block away at Bouchon Bakery. Specialty sand- wiches are $6.99; others $5.75. Many pasta salads to pick from, too. Annie the Baker cookies, produced locally, are also for sale. The coffee and espresso bar jolts sleepy eyes open starting at 6 a.m. daily and serves breakfast pastries, bagels, doughnuts, and egg sandwiches. The deli is in the Ranch Market Too building, with its own entrance, and access to the market. Closing time is 3 p.m.

Boysen Was a Berry Wizard

Legend has it that the boysenberry—a fruit created by crossing blackberries with loganberries and raspberries—originated in Napa Valley. Horticulturist Charles Rudolph Boysen attempted his berry-mingling alchemy in Napa in the 1920s, and brought forth a new hybrid that successfully bore fruit. But unable to achieve commercial success, he abandoned the effort. Some time later, Boysen moved to southern California, bringing along his newfangled berry vines, and went to work in Anaheim as parks superintendent. A fellow grower in Orange County named Walter Knott heard about Boysen's berry and tracked him down. The vines weren't doing so well, but Knott coaxed them back to good health. By 1935, Knott was robustly cultivating and selling the new berry, which he had named "boysenberry." In fact, Walter and his wife, Cordelia, were growing several crops successfully on their 20-acre farm, so much so that Cordelia opened a tea room to market the family's homemade jams and jellies. She later expanded into selling her fried chicken, homemade biscuits, and fresh-baked pies stuffed with a curious new fruit: boysenberries. Word spread about Cordelia's outstanding meals, and the Knott family farm in Buena Park, California, became a local sensation. Knott's Berry Farm, as it was eventually named, went on to become America's first theme park. It remains popular today, due in large part to the fruit Walter Knott named after Charles Rudolph Boysen's wizardry with the berry vines: the boysenberry.

Made or Grown Here

Full Table Farm, Yountville, CA 94599; (707) 944-8204; www .fulltablefarm.com. A small farm run by a husband and wife, the produce is sold primarily to local restaurants. In 2011 they were planning to sell their vegetables at local farmers' markets, too. Call Mindy for more information, or follow her updates on Facebook.

Food & Wine Pairings/ Landmark Wineries

Domaine Chandon, 1 California Dr., Yountville, CA 94599; (888) 242-6366; www.chandon.com. Established in the early 1970s by France's Moët et Chandon, Domaine Chandon was the first French-owned sparkling wine producer in Napa Valley. Known primarily for its bubbly (don't call it Champagne unless it really does come from Champagne, in France), Chandon also bottles still wines such as Chardonnay and Pinot Noir. Chandon is an example of a large, corporate winery that strives to appeal to all, with several tasting and tour options, art exhibits, and more. There's nothing wrong with that—if you have time to "do" only one winery, Chandon may be the perfect fit. The wine-tasting lounge serves a menu of goodies that would make a great midday meal or before-dinner snack, with options such as mixed olives or mixed nuts, caviar, *foie gras,* an artisanal cheese board, oysters on the half shell, and more. Open daily from 10 a.m. to 5 p.m.

Goosecross Cellars, 1119 State Ln., Yountville, CA 94599; (707) 944-1986 or (800) 276-9210; www.goosecross.com. The opposite of a winery experience such as Domaine Chandon (previous listing) is Goosecross, a small-production family winery that bottles several varietals, including Cabernet Sauvignon, Pinot Noir, Merlot, Chardonnay, Viognier, and Zinfandel. Estate winegrowing tours are conducted between June and October for visitors to experience the growing conditions and vineyard management techniques up-close and to explore the intricacies of winemaking. The tour concludes with a private tasting of wine. Open daily from 10 a.m. to 4:30 p.m.—please call ahead before dropping by.

Somerston Wine Co., 6490 Washington St., Yountville, CA 94599; (707) 944-8200; www.somerstonwineco.com. Three labels and numerous wine varietals are poured and sold here, most produced from grapes grown on the 1,600-acre Somerston Ranch, high in the eastern hills above Napa Valley. A flight of wines with cheese pairing is $40 per person; a cheese plate with dried fruit and nuts is available, too, along with a plate of chocolates made by local chocolate chef Chris Kollar. Much of the exposed wood you see inside this attractive tasting room in Yountville came from Somerston Ranch, repurposed into flooring and beams. Note the huge photo on the wall—that's a view of the ranch, where you can also take in spectacular vistas in an open-air ATV tour through vineyards and forests ($50) that concludes with a wine tasting. The ranch has approximately 200 acres of vineyards; 1,500 head of Dorper sheep overseen by a Peruvian sheepherder; and 10 acres of gardens with fruit and olive trees, vegetables, and herbs. In 2011, a natural soda spring on the ranch was tapped to bottle the healing waters, and for selling to the public at the ranch and at the Yountville tasting room. Somerston sells the seasonal produce it grows on the ranch, along with cheese and other items, in the space next door to the tasting room. The tasting room is open Tues through Sat from 11 a.m. to 9 p.m., and Sun and Mon from 1 to 8 p.m. See Somerston Ranch's recipe for **Lamb Kebabs with Cilantro Mint Pesto** on p. 233.

Oakville & Rutherford

Along this stretch of Napa Valley you'll see mostly vineyards, sprinkled with some of the big-name wineries in the region such as Opus One, Robert Mondavi, Franciscan, Francis Ford Coppola's Rubicon Estate, and Beaulieu. Oakville and Rutherford are unincorporated townships known not so much for food and dining but for their wine heritage and separate designations as American viticultural areas (AVAs). Approximately 2 miles apart, they have a combined population of about 800 residents.

As you can guess, Oakville earned its name from the thick groves of oak trees that grew in the vicinity. "Rutherford" came from Thomas Rutherford, the husband of the granddaughter of George Yount (see the Yountville chapter). As a wedding gift, George gave the couple more than a thousand acres of his Rancho Caymus land grant, and Thomas went on to develop a fine reputation as a grape-grower.

In the 1860s, Rutherford also became a water stop for a steam train operated by the Napa Valley Railroad Company. Sam Brannan founded the railroad to transport tourists between his resort of Calistoga to the north (see the Calistoga chapter) and the ferryboats that plied the waters out of Vallejo to the south. The same route now carries the modern-day Napa Valley Wine Train, a traveling restaurant you might see gliding along the tracks as it parallels the west side of Highway 29 and crosses over the road north of Rutherford at Whitehall Lane.

Rutherford has bragging rights to its "dust," which the vintners claim is the secret to the great Cabernet Sauvignon grapes grown in this AVA (also known as an appellation), and its "bench," generally considered to be the heart of Napa Valley's ultra-premium wine-grape acreage. The dust (soil) is gravelly, sandy, and loamy, and the Rutherford appellation receives more sun exposure than other parts of the Valley. These factors and many others create the chemistry necessary to produce the type of delicious Cabs that command the big dollars.

Dining and shopping options are limited in Oakville and Rutherford, but what's here is exceptional. Keep reading.

Landmark Eateries

Auberge du Soleil, 180 Rutherford Hill Rd., Rutherford, CA 94573; (707) 963-1211 or (800) 348-5406; www.aubergedusoleil.com; $$$$.

The "inn of the sun" was famous for being a restaurant before it became famous for being an exclusive 33-acre resort, and it's a current member of the France-based Relais & Chateaux association of luxury inns and restaurants worldwide. I consider Auberge du Soleil a splurge restaurant, with its beautiful hillside setting and Michelin-awarded cuisine (one star in 2011) suitable for a special occasion—a wedding proposal, a wedding anniversary, a milestone birthday, a soiree to celebrate your company going public. You get the idea. The enormous terrace looks out onto the rural beauty of Napa Valley, the ideal environment for digging into squid-ink risotto with prosciutto and shrimp; or halibut with fennel and quail egg; or local suckling pig served with an orange glaze and asparagus. The 3-course menu is $98 per person, and the 4-course menu is $115, not including wine. The tasting menu is a 6-course meal with wine pairings for $204 with wine, or $140 without. Lunch prices range from $29 to $42 for entrees such as sautéed chicken and a veal and lobster sandwich. Reservations are strongly recommended for the main restaurant, which is open daily at 7 a.m. for breakfast, switching to lunch at 11:30 a.m. (Mon through Fri). Brunch is served on weekends from 11:30 a.m. to 2:30 p.m., and dinner is every day from 5:30 to 9:30 p.m. The resort's less expensive and more casual Bistro & Bar ($$) is distinctive for the repurposed tree in the middle of the room that rises like a mast up to the skylight in the ceiling. Also note the wine barrel staves that create the "railing" overhead. The wraparound deck is the ideal location for sipping a cocktail at sunset, or choose from more than 40 wines by the glass. Stay for the cuisine—small plates ranging from ahi tuna tartare to wild mushrooms in a red-wine glaze to a spiced lamb skewer with couscous tabbouleh. Several entrees are also on the menu, as are charcuterie and cheese plates. Ten desserts, including a baked-to-order cookie plate, round out the meal. The Bistro & Bar, open daily from 11 a.m. to 11 p.m., doesn't take reservations. Both restaurants are open to the public. The main restaurant underwent remodeling and renovation in spring 2011.

Foodie Faves

La Luna Market & Taqueria, 1153 Rutherford Rd., Rutherford, CA 94573; (707) 963-3211; www.lalunamarket.com; $. Considered by many hungry and hard-working locals (plus a few winery CEOs and high-end restaurant chefs) to be the best taqueria in Napa Valley, this Latin market serves burritos, tacos, quesadillas, tortas, and nachos from a counter in the back of the store. The Luna Lunch is a complete combo with rice, beans, and tortillas with the meat of your choice (*carne asada* or *al pastor,* carnitas, pollo, or beef head and beef tongue). The vegetarian version of the Luna Lunch is a chile relleno. In business for decades, La Luna Market has earned great reviews from such heavyweight magazines as *Martha Stewart Living* and *Travel + Leisure.* The *San Francisco Chronicle* has also rated

La Luna among its Top 20 Best Taquerias in the entire Bay Area. Parking on this congested road can be difficult, and there are only three or four small tables outside the store for diners. So most folks grab their take-out and take off, or find a nearby shady spot to wolf it down. The market is open weekdays from 7 a.m. to 7 p.m., and on weekends from 8 a.m. to 6 p.m. (But don't be late—the kitchen stops cooking 30 minutes before closing time.)

Rutherford Grill, 1180 Rutherford Rd., Rutherford, CA 94573; (707) 963-1792; www.hillstone.com; $$. The Beverly Hills–based Hillstone Restaurant Group runs Rutherford Grill, but don't hold the corporate parentage against it. Open since 1994, the restaurant is like a roadhouse at a busy, busy corner (what is known locally as the Rutherford Cross Road, where Rutherford Road/Highway 128 junctions with Highway 29). Watch for the large palm trees in front of the building. The menu has changed little over the years because so many of the dishes are so popular. Although the Maytag blue cheese potato chips were finally retired (a great loss, in my opinion), the rotisserie chickens are still rotating slowly over the fire, thank goodness. Menu starters and sides include deviled eggs, a grilled jumbo artichoke, and skillet corn bread. The hacked chicken salad is sprinkled with some of that tasty rotisserie chicken.

Burgers, salads, and several entrees to choose from make for a satisfying meal at prices somewhat less than other popular Napa Valley spots. The wine list is heavy on reds from Napa and other California wine regions, with about 40 reds

Gourmet Dining on the Rails

The **Napa Valley Wine Train** harks back to another era, when the world moved at a slower pace and train travel could be romantic and intriguing, and usually included first-class dining. The Wine Train is lovely to watch as it rolls with grace past vineyards and wineries, providing its passengers with an unforgettable experience—a 3-hour, 36-mile round trip between the city of Napa and St. Helena, with a freshly prepared lunch or dinner along the way.

When the Wine Train began its daily journeys up and down the Valley more than 20 years ago, it added another dimension to dining here. Executive chef Kelly Macdonald uses local produce and sustainable meats and fish in his cuisine, all cooked onboard. The food is so beautifully presented at your table that it competes with the scenery outside.

The wine list is substantial, made up of many small-production labels not usually found outside the Valley. (Back at the train station in downtown Napa, the wine shop there is one of the best around, with more than 500 labels to choose from.)

Several trip options are offered in addition to the standard lunch and dinner packages. One of the most popular is the **Grgich Hills** winery tour (see the listing for Grgich Hills in this chapter). Vintner lunches, a murder mystery dinner theater trip, and an onboard wine tasting bar are also available.

Detailed information about the Napa Valley Wine Train and its various dining packages and extras can be found online at www.winetrain.com, or call (800) 427-4124. Reservations are a must.

and whites by the glass. Better still, bring your own bottle—there is no corkage fee. Rutherford Grill is open daily for lunch and dinner (to 10:30 p.m. weekends).

Specialty Stores & Markets

Oakville Grocery, 7856 St. Helena Hwy. (Hwy. 29), Oakville, CA 94562; (707) 944-8802; www.oakvillegrocery.com. On the outside, Oakville Grocery is a true blast from the past—a small rural store in business for more than 120 years, listed on the National Register of Historic Places, and still maintaining a colorful advertisement for Coca-Cola on its southern exterior. Inside, the fare is quite a bit different from whatever was available in 1890. Some call the store touristy and overpriced. I call it classic, the type of place you should drop into at least once if it's your first time in Napa Valley. The selection of fresh and packaged food makes the grocery popular, and so crowded at times it's difficult to turn around. But that's part of the fun. Benches and wine barrel tables outside can be used for munching on, perhaps, a meaty salami and provolone sandwich on a baguette. Baked goods, cheese, crackers, charcuterie, soft drinks and juices, jars of mustard, bottles of olive oil, bottles of wine— it's all here, and most is California-produced. Watch for limousines pulling in and out of the dusty parking lot. Oakville Grocery is also known for its catering business and the cool gift baskets it pulls together, which can be arranged online.

St. Helena Olive Oil Company, 8576 St. Helena Hwy. (Hwy. 29), Napa, CA 94558; (707) 697-1003; www.sholiveoil.com. Olive trees are grown in abundance in Napa Valley, as you will see if you do much driving around, and most of the olives are harvested by hand and pressed into oil. There's an oil production facility in this building, which was once a tractor manufacturing business way back when. Farmers would congregate in places like this, practically within shouting distance of the century-old Grange, just down the highway. The building was restored in 2001 to produce and sell olive oil products, pasta sauces, and other culinary items. Take the time to savor the oil and vinegar tastings and ask questions about using them in meal preparation. If you like dirty martinis, pick up a bottle of olive juice, a key ingredient in that cocktail. St. Helena Olive Oil Company has a second location in downtown St. Helena—see that chapter. (Note that the physical address above says Napa, but this store is in Rutherford at the intersection of Rutherford Road/Highway 128.)

Food & Wine Pairings/ Landmark Wineries

Beaulieu Vineyards, 1960 St. Helena Hwy. (Hwy. 29), Rutherford, CA 94573; (707) 967-5233 or (800) 264-6918; www.bvwines.com. Beaulieu gets major points for being historic—the oldest continually producing winery in Napa Valley. It got its name from the French founder's wife, who exclaimed "beau lieu!" ("beautiful place") when she saw the original property. But for almost as long as it's been in business the locals have referred to it as "BV"—and that's the dominant graphic element on its label. When many other wineries were forced out of business during Prohibition, Beaulieu soldiered on, making sacramental wine for churches. It turned out to be a good gig, and the winery's production had soared to more than a million gallons a year by the time Prohibition was repealed in 1933. After that the quality of their product took a major leap forward, and by the 1940s was good enough to be served at the White House. Today Beaulieu bottles both red and white wines. The reds include Cabernet Sauvignon, Merlot, Pinot Noir, Zinfandel, and a couple of blends. The whites are Chardonnay, Sauvignon Blanc, Pinot Grigio, Viognier, and a dessert Muscat. The winery is open daily from 10 a.m. to 5 p.m. for walk-in tastings.

Cakebread Cellars, 8300 St. Helena Hwy. (Hwy. 29), Rutherford, CA 94573; (800) 588-0298; www.cakebread.com. With a name like Cakebread, this winery is a natural for food-oriented tours and tastings. Cakebread loves to educate its visitors about pairing food with wine, particularly how certain wines do not go well with certain foods. Fortunately, you can get the lowdown during a 90-minute mini-tour and interactive food-and-wine pairing ($40 per person) that concentrates on four tastes of wine matched to four tastes of food, with ingredients taken from the winery's extensive vegetable gardens. The groups are kept small, and the classes are conducted 3 days a week with prior reservations. When Cakebread's

¾-acre garden is spilling over with excess produce, owner Dolores Cakebread might have her farm stand set up to share the bounty with visitors. Cakebread bottles several varietals, including Cabernet Sauvignon, Chardonnay, Sauvignon Blanc, Pinot Noir, Syrah, Zinfandel, and Merlot. All tours and tastings at Cakebread are by appointment only, so call first to inquire about reservations. The winery is also renowned for its regular cooking classes, which are usually sell-outs (see Learn to Cook in this chapter).

Franciscan Oakville Estate, 1178 Galleron Rd., Rutherford, CA 94573; (707) 967-3830 or (707) 967-3993; www.franciscan .com. Back when this winery was founded, its first notable release was a 1975 Cabernet Sauvignon. Franciscan went on to develop Magnificat, a blend of red Bordeaux varietals, leading the way for more "meritage" wines (the word marries "merit" to "heritage") from other wineries in Napa Valley. You can stop in here with no reservations to wine-taste only (unless you have a big group), for $15 per person. Two instructive seminars are offered daily at Franciscan that require advance reservations: one for learning how to blend wine ($40), and the other a sensory evaluation tutorial that's all about the "nose," the aroma of wine (also $40). Private wine experiences with cheese and other munchies can also be arranged, starting at $30 per person. Franciscan bottles several other varietals, such as Merlot, Chardonnay, Sauvignon Blanc, and Cuvée Sauvage, a Chardonnay that's barrel fermented with 100 percent wild yeast. They also make a white blend called Fountain Court (mostly Sauvignon Blanc), available only at the winery and named for the distinctive fountain in front of the tasting room entrance. Open daily from 10 a.m. to 5 p.m.

Grgich Hills Cellar, 1829 St. Helena Hwy. (Hwy. 29), Rutherford, CA 94573; (800) 532-3057; www.grgich.com. If you've heard of the "Judgment of Paris Tasting" of 1976, then you probably know about Miljenko "Mike" Grgich. Forty years ago, Mike was the winemaker at **Chateau Montelena** (see the Calistoga chapter) who helped create the remarkable 1973 Chardonnay that beat out all the other white wines in a blind tasting conducted by an all-French panel of judges in Paris. Mike received worldwide recognition for this achievement, and went on to start his own namesake winery in 1977. He continues to make award-winning Chardonnay, and bottles several other varietals as well: Fumé Blanc, Zinfandel, Cabernet Sauvignon, Merlot, and a dessert wine he calls "Violetta" in honor of his daughter. Now in his late 80s, Mike can still be seen doing business around the winery wearing his trademark beret. He was inducted into the Vintners Hall of Fame in 2008 and received a lifetime achievement award at the California State Fair that same year. Mike's winery is open daily for walk-in wine tasting from 9:30 a.m. to 4:30 p.m. With prior reservations, a private wine-and-cheese pairing is offered for $60 per person; the Library tour and tasting with cheese spotlights older vintages, for $75 per person. (For future reference, the Napa Valley Wine Train has a daily lunch and a Saturday night dinner option for passengers to first experience a tour and tasting with fruit-and-cheese pairings at Grgich, then hop the train right in front of the winery for their onboard meal.)

Mumm Napa Valley, 8445 Silverado Trail, Rutherford, CA 94573; (707) 967-7700 or (800) 686-6272; www.mummnapa.com. Back in the late 1970s, the French Champagne producer G.H. Mumm began an exhaustive search for the ideal winegrowing region in America to make sparkling wine. Napa Valley was the lucky winner. By 1986, Mumm had completed construction of this winery along a picturesque portion of the Silverado Trail. Besides its bubbly, Mumm Napa is noted for a spacious patio, and also the rotating photography exhibits in a museumlike gallery. The Ansel Adams collection of classic, stunning black-and-white photography is permanent, while other presentations come and go (such as photos of music legends shot by Baron Wolman for *Rolling Stone* magazine). For $65, enjoy two flutes of rare wines matched with fruit and artisanal cheeses, all while looking out over the remarkable view. This food pairing is by appointment only, while walk-ins are welcome for wine tasting only from 10 a.m. to 4:45 p.m. daily.

Opus One, 7900 St. Helena Hwy. (Hwy. 29), Oakville, CA 94562; (707) 944-9442 or (800) 292-6787; www.opusonewinery.com. The wine is in a class by itself, the building magnificent. Opus One is a singular red wine, a blend that's 79 percent Cabernet Sauvignon and developed from a joint venture between America's Robert Mondavi and France's Baron Philippe de Rothschild. When Opus One came to market in 1984, it was considered America's first ultra-premium wine—meaning any wine priced at $50 or more per bottle. (The current vintage retails for $200 per bottle, and purchases are capped at six bottles because of its limited production.) The winery was completed in 1991 with a mixture of European and California design elements. It's one of those structures that when seen from a distance for the first time, you might mutter, "What is that?" The cream-colored Texas limestone blends well with the brilliant green of the surrounding vineyards. Inside it's somewhat formal, reflecting the influence of the European co-founder. All visits are by appointment only. Reservations for the 75-minute tour of the estate and a tasting ($50 per person) cannot be made online, so you must call ahead. Because the winery produces only one wine, a tasting-only of Opus One (no tour) costs $35. Reservations for tasting are also required, and can be arranged online.

Robert Mondavi Winery, 7801 St. Helena Hwy. (Hwy. 29), Oakville, CA 94562; (888) 766-6328; www.robertmondavi.com. Robert Mondavi was so famous for so many decades that to describe him as an "icon" is too clichéd. The man was a master at drawing visitors to Napa Valley and making an impact in the wine world, yet he was also a philanthropist, giving back to the community at every opportunity. He's gone now, and the winery is owned by a huge alcoholic beverage company, but it's still a quintessential wine-country experience, particularly for first-time visitors. The options for food-and-wine pairing include the Harvest of Joy tour and lunch ($100 per person, Wed and Sun), when Mondavi's signature wines are poured during a 3-course feast in the winery's Vineyard Room. Less expensive are the wine-and-chocolate and wine-and-cheese pairings (each is $50 per person on Sat and Sun). Go for the full treatment and gather together a few friends for the Four Decades tasting experience ($300 per person), a complete dinner matched with Mondavi wines from the past 4 decades (pre-corporate take-over). All of these food pairings require prior reservations. The many Robert Mondavi-bottled varietals include Cabernet Sauvignon, Fumé Blanc, Chardonnay, Pinot Noir, and Merlot. Open daily from 10 a.m. to 5 p.m.

Round Pond Estate, 886 Rutherford Rd., Rutherford, CA 94573; (888) 302-2575; www.roundpond.com. You could sit on the 2nd-story terrace here and watch the view for hours—one of the best unobstructed vistas from a winery in the entire Valley. The easiest way to make that happen is to reserve a food-and-wine pairing, available daily between 11 a.m. and 3:30 p.m. by appointment. The choices include the estate wine tasting ($25 per person), featuring three wines and three appetizers, while the guided tour and tasting ($35) takes place at 11 a.m. daily with several tastes of wine and bites of wine-friendly food. Round Pond is diverse, producing wine, olive oils, and red-wine vinegars. Their more elaborate food-and-wine pairings incorporate all of those ingredients and more. From

May to Oct, the winery hosts alfresco lunches, scheduled Mon through Sat at 12:30 p.m. ($65 per person). After a garden tour and a guided tasting of the wines, olive oils, and vinegars, participants sit down for a lunch of cheese, meats, bread, fruits, and vegetables from the estate garden, and dessert. For a bit more ($75), sign up for the garden-to-table brunch (on Sun from May to Oct). That's the garden tour and lunch with a few extras included, such as a cooking demonstration and a discussion about food-and-wine pairings. Once during the harvest season, Round Pond offers the Day in the Life experience ($200 per person), lasting approximately 6 hours. After a light breakfast, guests participate in picking wine grapes, sorting and helping to press the grapes, and learning some of the science behind winemaking. That's followed by instruction in food-and-wine pairing and a gourmet lunch. Perhaps you'd prefer to skip the dusty work in the vineyard and go directly to the once-monthly, $250-per-person multicourse gourmet dinner paired with Round Pond wines. All of these experiences require advance reservations. Round Pond produces Cabernet Sauvignon and Sauvignon Blanc; red-wine vinegars made from Sangiovese, Nebbiolo, and Petit Verdot; blood orange and Meyer lemon citrus syrups; and an assortment of premium olive oils. A 90-minute tour of the olive mill, which makes the golden nectar from the estate's olive trees, is also available three times daily ($35 per person). All tours and tastings at Round Pond are by appointment only. The facility is reached down a long, palm tree–lined driveway. See Chef Hannah

Bauman's recipe for **Meyer Lemon & Ancho Chile Chicken** on p. 242.

Rubicon Estate Winery, 1991 St. Helena Hwy. (Hwy. 29), Rutherford, CA 94573; (707) 968-1161 or (800) RUBICON; www .rubiconestate.com. It's the famous owner, the Hollywood connection, that brings the curious to Rubicon. Movie director Francis Ford Coppola has owned this property since the 1970s and has spent millions of dollars restoring the historic buildings. Rubicon is Coppola's signature product, a blend of Cabernet Sauvignon, Merlot, and Cabernet Franc that's ideal for putting away in the cellar to save for a special event. Coppola's proprietary white wine is called Blancaneaux, a blend of Marsanne, Roussanne, and Viognier. He also bottles Zinfandel, Marsanne, Merlot, and Syrah. Several tasting experiences are offered at Rubicon. The Daniel tasting ($25) includes a flight of five wines, while the Coppola tasting ($50) is a seated gathering with bread and cheese. Other tastings require advance reservations, such as the hour-long Amuse tasting ($45) with pork *rillettes* and other bites of food paired with three of the estate wines. The Elevage Experience ($75) lasts 2 hours and is capped by a seated wine tasting of barrel samples together with a platter of gourmet cheese. Some tastings include a 30-minute walking tour of the property. The winery is open daily from 10 a.m. to 5 p.m. In a recent business deal, Coppola acquired the name Inglenook, the estate's one-time name that represents a long winemaking heritage at this site. He plans to call Rubicon Estate "Inglenook" from now on, but the filmmaker is a busy man and the name conversion might not be noticed by visitors for some time. (Coppola once had a collection of memorabilia from his films on display at Rubicon, but the five Academy Award statuettes and the desk and chair from *The Godfather*—among many other movie treasures—have been relocated to his namesake Sonoma County winery.)

Rutherford Hill Winery, 200 Rutherford Hill Rd., Rutherford, CA 94573; (707) 963-1871; www.rutherfordhill.com. This winery is noteworthy for two reasons: its extensive cave system for storing and aging wine, and the charming picnic groves that overlook Napa Valley. Lots of wineries have caves, but this system extends for nearly a mile and includes a dining room for events. At any given time, approximately 8,000 wine barrels are stacked in the caves, which maintain a consistent temperature of 59 degrees F and 90 percent humidity. Outside, the picnic tables are available on a first-come, first-served basis for visitors who've already taken a tour or tasted the wines. No reservations are required for the tours, which are conducted daily at 11:30 a.m., 1:30 p.m., and 3:30 p.m. Another reason for visiting Rutherford Hill is the Blend Your Own Merlot seminar, conducted on Saturday. In addition to an in-depth tour and private wine tasting, you learn sensory evaluation skills to make your own individual blend that can be bottled with a cork and a personalized label. Call the winery for prices of the tours and the blending class. Open daily from 10 a.m. to 5 p.m.

St. Supery Vineyards, 8440 St. Helena Hwy. (Hwy. 29), Rutherford, CA 94573; (707) 963-4507 or (800) 942-0809; www.stsupery.com. Repeat after me: Smell-a-vision. It's what makes wine tasting a bit more fun at St. Supery. Smell-a-vision is an interactive display that tests your nose for sniffing out the flavors and the aromas in wine. If you've come for the food pairings, every Saturday at 11 a.m. the winery features either a wine-and-cheese seminar with gourmet hors d'oeuvres matched to the estate Cabernet Sauvignons, or a chocolate pairing (each is $40 per person). Both of these pairings require prior reservations. St. Supery bottles many varietals, with its Sauvignon Blanc lately leading the pack and earning positive reviews. There is also Cabernet Sauvignon, Merlot, Malbec, a Bordeaux blend called Elu, Semillon, and Chardonnay. Open daily from 10 a.m. to 5 p.m.

Sequoia Grove Winery, 8338 St. Helena Hwy. (Hwy. 29), Napa, CA 94558; (707) 944-2945; www.sequoiagrove.com. Named for the grove of sequoia trees in which it stands, this winery cares less about putting on airs and more about giving visitors a happy experience. Perhaps it's the enormous redwood trees that make it unique—here on the Valley floor there are precious few of those behemoths to be found. The tree theme continues in the tasting room, with the bar carved from a single slab of a giant tree. The mood is looser here than in most tasting rooms you'll visit nearby. Sequoia Grove produces several varietals, some available only at the winery, and at least one limited-production port. Call ahead for reservations, pricing, and details about the wine-and-chocolate pairing, when the winery matches its Cabernet Sauvignon to several confections made by local chocolatiers. A wine-and-cheese pairing is also offered. Occasionally, Sequoia Grove hosts an inexpensive barbecue luncheon or other food-focused happening that requires advance reservations. Check the website under "Events" for the latest. Sequoia Grove is open daily for walk-in wine tasting from 10:30 a.m. to 5 p.m. (Note that the physical address above is Napa—it's a US Postal Service quirk—but this tasting room is located in Rutherford.)

Silver Oak Cellars, 915 Oakville Crossroad, Oakville, CA 94562; (707) 944-8808 or (800) 273-8809; www.silveroak.com. The tasting room was completely rebuilt after a fire a few years ago into a stunning new facility—the better to savor this winery's one product: Cabernet Sauvignon. Silver Oak's red elixir is the type that can be cellared for decades and will still taste great when you pull the cork to celebrate, say, the day the United States colonizes Mars (if you really want to wait that long). Silver Oak bucked tradition in the early 1970s by choosing to age its wines in American oak barrels, not French oak, and today it owns several hundred acres of white oak timberland in Missouri for crafting into barrels. Current releases of Silver Oak wines can be tasted daily for $20 per person (and you keep the logo glass). Other tours and tastings require reservations, such as the food-and-wine pairing on weekdays at 2 p.m., with special nibbles created by winery chef Dominic Orsini (a nice man). The winery is open Mon through Sat from 9 a.m. to 5 p.m., and Sun from 11 a.m. to 5 p.m.

Swanson Vineyards, 1271 Manley Ln., Rutherford, CA 94573; (707) 754-4018; www.swansonvineyards.com. Familiar with Swanson frozen food? This winery was founded by members of that famous TV-dinner family, so they should know something about food pairings. While many of the wineries in Napa Valley are steeped in history and exude a masculine vibe, the newbie Swanson's tasting room experience seems almost girly by comparison. Instead of a gentlemen's club–style atmosphere, Swanson welcomes guests into its "Sip Shoppe," where informal tastings take place Thurs through Sun from 11 a.m. to 4 p.m., the winery's regular days and hours of operation. The Sip Shoppe has been described as a cross between an art gallery, a candy store, and a French Quarter parlor. With sultry French ballads on the sound system and the walls and ceiling covered in red stripes, tasters sit at picnic tables and are treated to a potato chip topped with a dollop of domestic caviar and crème fraîche paired with Swanson's Pinot Grigio and Chardonnay ($15 per person). A more expensive tasting ($25) matches the winery's Cabernet Sauvignon and Angelica dessert wine with curry-rolled chocolate and Castello blue cheese. Another option is to combine sips of Petite Sirah and Semillon with blue cheese and hot pistachio nuts ($22). As a palate refresher during the experience, you might be served the Dizzy Lizzy Sno Ball, an Italian ice drizzled with Pinot Grigio. In addition to the Swanson family, one of the business partners in the Sip Shoppe is Andy Spade, husband of fashion designer Kate Spade and brother of comedian David Spade.

ZD Wines, 8383 Silverado Trail, Napa, CA 94558; (800) 487-7757; www.zdwines.com. ZD is a multigenerational family business, first founded in 1969 by two former aerospace engineers, Norman deLeuze and Gino Zepponi. Norman's children and grandchildren continue to run the place, and Norman's widow, Rosa Lee, is the inspiration for the winery's "Rosa Lee's Whim" label. One year her whim could be the Syrah grape, the next Barbera. (The 2010 Rosa Lee's Whim is a Pinot Grigio.) ZD is also known for its Cabernet Sauvignon, Pinot Noir, and Chardonnay. To educate visitors in the pairing of food and wine, the Vineyard View tasting ($40 per person) includes a selection of three or four ZD wines matched with artisanal

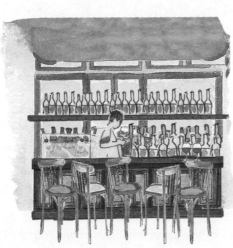

cheese and a chocolate truffle. This pairing takes place on Sun at 11 a.m. and Mon through Fri by appointment. To attract bicyclists, ZD also hosts a Sunday morning 6-mile bike ride called the Eco Tour (summer only) that focuses on organic winemaking and concludes with a delicious breakfast made with organic ingredients. Walk-in tasters are always welcome, too, during the winery's regular daily hours of 10 a.m. to 4:30 p.m. (The US Postal Service insists on giving this winery a Napa zip code, but it's actually east of Rutherford.)

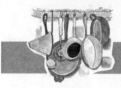

Learn to Cook

Cakebread Cellars, 8300 St. Helena Hwy. (Hwy. 29), Rutherford, CA 94573; (800) 588-0298; www.cakebread.com. About once a month, Cakebread conducts a hands-on cooking class open to the public. Depending on the season, students will be indoors in the winery's professionally equipped kitchen or preparing the meal at the outdoor barbecue with a wood-burning oven. The classes usually start at 9:30 a.m. with a tour of the property and a wine tasting, followed by the class and the 3-course lunch you've helped to prepare. All this and a Cakebread Cellars logo apron, too, for $175 per person. Some of the classes in 2011 went in-depth into summertime grilling, the basics of cooking seafood, putting grown-up spins on childhood comfort foods, and making cassoulet. Reservations are required, of course.

St. Helena

More than a few people have compared St. Helena's Main Street to Beverly Hills' Rodeo Drive. There are some similarities, but on a smaller scale—and minus Rodeo's flower-filled median strip and towering palm trees. (And St. Helena is surrounded by thousands of acres of fresh air and rural agriculture, instead of hundreds of square miles of a noisy, smoggy megalopolis.) So as you stroll Main Street's sidewalks, a John Deere tractor might bounce past on its way to a nearby vineyard, or a big rig hauling wine grapes is likely to rumble by slowly. After all, Main Street is Highway 29, the major traffic artery through Napa Valley, and it's a narrow two lanes wide here. However, you will still see plenty of limousines and town cars, just as in Beverly Hills.

An English doctor named Edward Bale is credited with opening up the settlement of this region of Napa Valley to American pioneers. In 1841 Bale received a huge land grant from the Mexican administrator of the territory, and by the mid-1850s there were homes and small businesses going up along Main Street. (The town is named after the large mountain to the north, St. Helena, pronounced "hel-LAY-na," overlooking Calistoga.) The early farmers soon determined the soil was ideal for growing grapes, and the wine industry was off and running. Even a century ago, St. Helena was attracting vacationers who enjoyed the European-style town with its large population of German, Swiss, and French inhabitants.

Today's city fathers and mothers are protective of St. Helena's historic legacy and its cozy, small-town ambience (population 5,814). Yet it's still drawing visitors from around the globe who seek a charming rural community with first-class dining and shopping, and abundant wine culture. By the way, when you hear locals referring to the "CIA" in conversation, they aren't talking about our nation's spooky undercover intelligence agency—they mean the Culinary Institute of America, on the north edge of town.

Landmark Eateries

Cindy's Backstreet Kitchen, 1327 Railroad Ave., St. Helena, CA 94574; (707) 963-1200; www.cindysbackstreetkitchen.com; $$. Cindy's is one of Chef Cindy Pawlcyn's three restaurants in Napa Valley. The first place she opened was **Mustards Grill** (see the Yountville chapter), and the second was this eatery a block off Main Street. (Her third restaurant is **Brassica,** listed in this chapter's Foodie Faves.) The building that houses Cindy's is more than a 100 years old and has seen many uses over the years. The restaurant's interior has a sweet farmhouse feel to it, with seating on two floors and outside. The full bar makes a fine before-dinner diversion to savor a special cocktail, such as the Railroad Mary or the Sidecar Named Desire. Then it's on to the main event—Cindy's cuisine. Regular customers swear by the Chinatown duck burger, meat loaf, mushroom tamales, Vietnamese lettuce wraps, roasted artichoke, and other menu classics. On special weeknights, Cindy's Supper Club options might be penne carbonara with asparagus tips, pancetta, and egg; mustard-braised rabbit with mushrooms and buttered noodles; or Tunisian poached fish with olives, preserved lemons, and capers. End the meal with a piece of campfire pie to share with the table—it's enormous. Cindy's is popular with locals and visitors, and celebrities, too, when they're in town: Natalie Portman dined here with her fiancé just days after winning her 2011 Academy Award for Best Actress. Open daily for lunch and dinner.

The Restaurant at Meadowood, 900 Meadowood Ln., St. Helena, CA 94574; (707) 967-1205; www.meadowood.com; $$$$. Along with Thomas Keller of the French Laundry in Yountville, Christopher Kostow is the other chef in the San Francisco Bay Area to have earned three stars for his restaurant in the 2011 *Michelin Guide*. It's a major achievement, and Christopher keeps wowing diners with spectacular California cuisine. Serving dinner only, Mon through Sat, the restaurant offers a 4-course tasting menu ($125 per person) and a chef's tasting menu ($225 per person). Wine pairings are extra. Some of the building blocks Christopher uses to construct his innovative dishes include Waygu beef, Monterey Bay abalone, local guinea hens, and sea cucumbers. The menu changes with the seasons and availability of fresh produce, as well as what's ready to harvest in the restaurant's garden. Each plate brought to the table is a work of art, assembled with flair and imagination. The restaurant has approximately 70 seats indoors and out (when the weather is fine, ask for a table on the terrace). The service is top drawer, professional and friendly. Diners are expected to dress accordingly for this upscale experience, although jackets for men are not absolutely necessary. If you're wearing denim, however, please make it a dark shade. Meadowood is a luxury resort, where presidents have slept and where the annual Auction Napa Valley takes place. It's reached up a narrow lane off Silverado Trail.

Terra and Bar Terra, 1345 Railroad Ave., St. Helena, CA 94574; (707) 963-8931; www.terrarestaurant.com; $$$$ in the main restaurant, $$ in Bar Terra. A longtime favorite of locals and visitors, housed in a large stone building, Terra was updated in 2011 with a full bar (to the right when you walk in the door), to balance the small formal dining room to the left. Chef-Owners Hiro Sone and Lissa Doumani revamped the menu offerings, too. The chefs create cuisine reflecting the tastes of southern France and northern Italy, but with Japanese twists (example: sake-marinated cod and shrimp dumplings with shiso broth). In the dining room you can choose from a tasting menu of 3 to 6 courses ($57 to $92 per person). On any given night there could be 17 savory dishes to pick from (duck breast on a grilled peach, for instance) and six sweet plates (such as huckleberry pie with Meyer lemon ice cream). Bar Terra is a less expensive option to still enjoy Hiro and Lissa's cuisine. Snacks include a deviled egg with salmon caviar or spiced almonds. "In jar" spreadables might be duck liver mousse, pork *rillettes,* and fish tartare. Hiro and Lissa met when they were both working for Wolfgang Puck at Spago in Los Angeles. Eager to helm their own restaurant, they opened Terra in 1988 and have been gathering big-time praise ever since—Terra has been a Michelin award recipient for several years. Serving dinner only beginning at 6 p.m.; Bar Terra opens at 5:30 p.m.

Tra Vigne, 1050 Charter Oak Ave., St. Helena, CA 94574; (707) 964-4444; www.travignerestaurant.com; $$$. Celebrity chef Michael Chiarello founded Tra Vigne many years ago. He's moved on to other culinary pursuits (see the Yountville chapter), but this restaurant he created in St. Helena is still a draw, still lovely, and still serving excellent Italian cuisine with California influences. You will feel as if you've been transported to Italy in these Old World–style surroundings, so score a table on the patio if you can to enjoy the full alfresco experience. Forget about your latest cholesterol test and start the meal with fresh mozzarella made just for you. Other cold and hot antipasto options include a classic Caesar, rosemary pizzetta, and a baked fig pizza. Follow that with pasta and protein: sage-infused pappardelle, rigatoni alla carbonara, goat cheese ravioli, smoked and braised short ribs, wood oven–roasted rainbow trout, and local halibut are just a few of the options. Tra Vigne is open for lunch and dinner daily, and brunch on Sun.

Wine Spectator Restaurant at Greystone, Culinary Institute of America (CIA), 2555 Main St. (Hwy. 29), St. Helena, CA 94574; (707) 967-1010; www.ciachef.edu/greystonerestaurant; $$$. Normally I wouldn't recommend dining at a school, but this isn't just any school. It's the West Coast branch of the New York-based Culinary Institute of America. The CIA staffs this restaurant with its students and professional chef instructors, so the cuisine is top-notch and cutting edge. Remember, the CIA has graduated some big names in the foodie world, and the students in the kitchen when you dine here may also be on the road to greatness. In any case, you'll get a tasty meal, prepared in an open kitchen. The menu changes weekly to keep the students on their toes and offer diners a constantly evolving selection of dishes. A recent menu included for-the-table shared bites such as an olive oil tasting and oysters on the half-shell. First courses ranged from a roasted beet and kohlrabi salad to Monterey Bay sardines with baby artichokes and *salsa verde*. Mains were a crispy chicken confit, grilled hanger steak, and pan-roasted whole fish. Sides are extra but could be sautéed spinach and fingerling potatoes, or *horta,* a salad made of cooked rainbow chard and dressed with dill, garlic, feta cheese, lemon juice, and olive oil. Check the back of your menu for fun "did you know?" culinary trivia. The restaurant is open daily, and reservations are recommended. The first seating begins at 11:15 a.m. for lunch; the last seating of the day is usually at 9 p.m.

Brassica Mediterranean Kitchen and Wine Bar, 641 Main St. (Hwy. 29), St. Helena, CA 94574; (707) 963-0700; www.brassicanapa valley.com; $$$. Chef Cindy Pawlcyn shook things up in her three-restaurant empire in 2011 with the late summer opening of Brassica. For 5 years, the restaurant Cindy ran at this address was called Go Fish, specializing in seafood and sushi. For whatever reasons, chef/owners sometimes do an about-face in cuisine, but what Cindy has planned is sure to be successful. She has an amazing track record in Napa Valley (Mustards Grill and Cindy's Backstreet Kitchen), and Brassica will likely be a hit. (Cindy points out that Brassica is Latin for the family of plants that includes mustard.) Though the menu had not been unveiled when this book was completed, Cindy offered a few tidbits of information: The focus will be on wine-friendly, Mediterranean-style dishes, with influences from Italy, France, Spain, Greece, Morocco, and Turkey. Fans of by-the-glass wines are sure to be delighted—70 selections to choose, many from small producers, as well as 10 wines "on tap." The wine bar will offer the full food menu, along with cocktails. To create a new look for the new cuisine, the inside of the restaurant was also redesigned and updated. Open for lunch and dinner.

Cook, 1310 Main St. (Hwy. 29), St. Helena, CA 94574; (707) 963-7088; www.cooksthelena.com; $$. Cook has the cozy feel of a neighborhood joint, with at least 10 seats at the counter. The restaurant is popular for its braised short ribs, if you're in a red meat kind of mood, and the refreshing Meyer lemon cream tart for dessert when you have a sweet tooth that needs satisfying. Instead of trying to offer too many choices, the chef keeps it simple, with three or four options in each category of appetizers, salads, pastas, and entrees. These might be mussels or fried calamari; a daily soup; handmade mozzarella served with pesto, Meyer lemon oil and gray salt; Caesar salad; risotto of the day; pork pappardelle; fettuccine *vongole* (clams); and gnocchi with marinara or Gorgonzola cream. Meaty entrees are the whole young chicken, stuffed red trout, and a dry-aged rib eye with shoestring potatoes. The lunch menu lists most of the same dishes but with sandwiches added, like a porto-bello mushroom sandwich, a BLE (smoked bacon and organic eggs on focaccia, with fries), and a burger. Take note of the cool lighted sculpture on the wall. Open Tues through Sat for lunch and dinner; Sun for dinner only.

Farmstead Restaurant, 738 Main St. (Hwy. 29), St. Helena, CA 94574; (707) 963-9181; www.farmsteadnapa.com, or www.long meadowranch.com; $$. Farmstead is the restaurant business of the larger Hall family enterprise called **Long Meadow Ranch** (see listing in this chapter), producers of grass-fed beef, wine, extra-virgin olive oil, and other foods on a huge ranch up on the mountainside near Rutherford. The restaurant and wine-tasting complex that opened in fall 2009 at the corner of Main Street and Charter Oak Avenue offers several diversions. The restaurant was once a nursery barn, now smartly remodeled with a rustic-chic feel. The old farm implements look a bit menacing as wall and ceiling decor, but it's all in good fun. Many other repurposed materials were used in the remodeling, such as discarded redwood framing, tree stumps, rocks and granite, antique tools, and so forth. The outdoor seating area has rocking chairs and upholstered sofas, and the large patio offers beer and wine tasting. Don't miss the demonstration garden of herbs and vegetables, to stroll through at your leisure.

Sustainable, organic local ingredients are used in the cuisine, including meat and produce from Long Meadow Ranch. The chili with Rancho Gordo *pinquito* beans is a good way to start the meal, followed by brick-cooked chicken, or the grass-fed beef cut of the day (just ask). Try sitting at a community table so you can break bread with new friends. Corkage is only $2, donated to a local nonprofit that changes monthly. Open daily for lunch and dinner. (See Food & Wine Pairings for information about Long Meadow Ranch wines.)

Gillwood's Cafe, 1313 Main St. (Hwy. 29), St. Helena, CA 94574; (707) 963-1788; www.gillwoodscafe.com; $. Something you might learn the hard way, after indulging in too much of the grape late into the evening, is that your tummy craves hangover food the next morning. Gillwood's understands this and is open early to help you shake off the willies. It's St. Helena's favorite breakfast spot, and lunch is served, too. You may see a line of people eager for coffee and eggs waiting to get in, but the turnover of tables usually moves quickly. The egg scrambles with various ingredients (salmon with cream cheese and capers—yum) are popular, and big appetites might appreciate the breakfast casserole or the house-made corned-beef hash. The lunch menu can be counted on for standard cafe fare, such as burgers, cold sandwiches, grilled sandwiches, and a couple of soups. Craving greens? Try one of the tasty main-dish salads. Gillwood's celebrated its 20th anniversary in 2011 at this location; the Napa location is 6 years younger (1320 Napa Town Center, Napa, CA 94599; 707-253-0409). Open daily at 7 a.m., with breakfast served all day. Lunch service begins at 10:30 a.m., and closing time is 3 p.m.

Giugni's Deli, 1227 Main St. (Hwy. 29), St. Helena, CA 94574; (707) 963-3421; $. Foodies can be fanatical about their favorite delis. Matching meat, cheese, and bread together is deeply personal for sandwich lovers. That's why Giugni's gets high praise for staying true to its purpose—being a small-town delicatessen loved by locals and a "discovery" for visitors. When you step inside, the aroma of good fast food fills the air, a combination of whatever is simmering in the soup pot and the pungent mixture of smoked cheese and corned beef. Try the sopressata salami (wine cured) with smoked Swiss cheese on a hard sour roll, sprinkled with a generous helping of Giugni Juice, the deli's "secret" herb-infused vinaigrette (buy a bottle on your way out). With more than 25 meats, 20 cheeses, and about 14 types of fresh bread to choose from, you can try a new sandwich every time you walk in. Plenty of side salads, too, including artichoke hearts, and a refreshing marinated tomato-and-cucumber combo. Don't forget dessert: the selection of old-fashioned candies is impressive, with jawbreakers, lollipops, and much more. While waiting for your order, check out the old newspaper clippings and photos on the walls, and the interesting items for sale. The store is open from 9 a.m. to 5 p.m. daily.

Gott's Roadside Tray Gourmet, 933 Main St. (Hwy. 29), St. Helena, CA 94574; (707) 963-3486; www.gottsroadside.com; $. This roadside diner is also described in the City of Napa chapter, where it has a location at the Oxbow Public Market. The menu is the same at both places; the difference is the Oxbow location has indoor seating, which this location does not. Instead, there's a large lawn with umbrella-covered picnic tables—consider sharing yours with strangers. You order at a walk-up window, then wait for your food at a picnic table or take it to go. Someone on staff will usually come by to refill glasses and take away your trash, too. I rarely order onion rings at burger joints because I'm usually disappointed, but the rings at Gott's are the best—large, not too greasy, and easier to eat than most. And the milkshakes, well, they're worth the steep price ($5.99). This is the original Gott's, dating back decades (there's a third in San Francisco), and it still has the "Taylor's Refresher" sign out front, which is its former name. Most locals still refer to it as Taylor's, too, so when people recommend the ahi burger at Taylor's, they mean Gott's. Open 10:30 a.m. to 10 p.m. in summer, closing an hour earlier in winter.

Market, 1347 Main St. (Hwy. 29), St. Helena, CA 94574; (707) 963-3799; www.marketsthelena.com; $$. Comfort food, taken to the next level—that's how I've always described Market to visitors who want a recommendation for a decent place to eat that won't break the bank. Calling itself an "American restaurant," Market serves classics such as fried chicken (organic, of course), macaroni and cheese, fish-and-chips, a half-pound burger, lasagna, and filet mignon. If you're really hungry, splurge on the sides, like the onion rings or the cornbread. Generally speaking, to score a table right away it's best to wait until the lunch crowd has moved on (what those in the biz call "linner"—the time between lunch and dinner). On Sundays from 10 a.m. to 3 p.m., Market offers a breakfast menu along with its regular dishes. Expect huevos rancheros, a couple of different omelettes, corned-beef and Yukon-potato hash, eggs Benedict, and Belgian waffles. Open daily for lunch and dinner.

Pizzeria Tra Vigne, 1016 Main St. (Hwy. 29), St. Helena, CA 94574; (707) 967-9999; www.travignerestaurant.com/pizzeria .html; $. Look for the large tomato sculpture out front—that's the entrance to this pizzeria that's part of the Tra Vigne restaurant enterprise in St. Helena. If you have children in tow, a good pizza parlor can be a godsend. Pizzeria Tra Vigne can keep the kids happy while satisfying the adults, too. In addition to pizza (try the

"Vespa"), the house-made pasta comes five ways, along with anti-pasto options, salads, oven-baked sandwiches, *piadine* (flatbreads with salads on top), and gelato for dessert. For a pizza joint, the wine list is extensive, or you can select one of the house-label draft beers. The pizzeria is open daily for lunch and dinner.

Press, 587 St. Helena Hwy. (Hwy. 29), St. Helena, CA 94574; (707) 967-0550; www.pressthelena.com; $$$. Press is where diners go for a great dry-aged steak to match with hearty red wines. The interior is lovely, a farmhouse-like space filled with natural light. The 2011 *Michelin Guide* gave Press recognition as a recommended steakhouse. The prime Angus beef is cooked over cherry and almond wood in a custom-built grill and rotisserie. And give Press points for having a Bacon Bar as part of its less-expensive bar menu. Artisanal pork producers are spotlighted, with a bacon sampler plate available. The raw bar menu has seafood platters in two sizes, petite and grande. The main menu is mostly beef, but with salmon and chicken options for lighter appetites. The restaurant's wine list is huge, consisting exclusively of Napa Valley producers. Press is open for dinner every day except Tues, serving until 10 p.m.

Sogni di Dolci, 1142 Main St. (Hwy. 29), St. Helena, CA 94574; (707) 968-5257; www.sognididolci.com; $. With the exception of Gillwood's Cafe about a block away, there are few opportunities to score an early-morning breakfast on Main Street in St. Helena. Thank goodness for this place. Best known for having at least 18 flavors of gelato at any one time, Sogni di Dolci also serves light breakfasts, such as a ham, turkey, or pancetta panino with egg and cheese. Perhaps you'd prefer the scrambled egg and tomato panino. Focaccia toast with jam is also offered, along with a breakfast bruschetta, bagel with cream cheese, and assorted locally made pastries. There's espresso too, of course, to kick-start your day. It's difficult to choose between the many gelato flavors, but take a crack at blackberry Cabernet, green tea, or chocolate hazelnut with real hazelnut bits. For lunch or dinner, panini rule here. Get your focaccia stuffed in many ways: with prosciutto and mozzarella, or chicken and roasted peppers, ham, tuna, as a BLT, and others. The salads are crisp and fresh, from simple mixed greens to a toasted pecan and pear affair topped with shaved Parmesan cheese. Vegetarian choices are served also, along with a soup of the day and a Tuscan tomato variety. Sogni di Dolci opens at 6 a.m. most days (a bit later on weekends), and serves until 9 or 9:30 p.m. (closing earlier on Sun).

That Pizza Place, 1149 Main St. (Hwy. 29), St. Helena, CA 94574; (707) 968-9671; www.californiapizzashop.blogspot.com; $. Keeping it simple, the owners of That Pizza Place make only pizza in this small storefront at the north end of the Sunshine Foods shopping area right off Spring Street. There's seating for 12, but most people get their pies to go. Choose your own combination of toppings, or select from one of the specialties, such as the Hot & Sweet, with bacon, jalapeños, and pineapple. Open daily 10:30 a.m. to 9 p.m.

Villa Corona Cocina Mexicana, 1138 Main St. (Hwy. 29), St. Helena, CA 94574; (707) 963-7812; www.villacoronash.com; $. This budget-friendly, informal Mexican restaurant doesn't attempt "trendy," just authentic. Inside are Spanish-style wooden chairs and tables, with children's drawings under the glass tabletops. Expect about 15 varieties of the burrito, 12 combo platters, several seafood options, and breakfast platters, too. There's some outside seating, if you don't mind being close to slow-moving traffic. Open Mon through Sat from 9 a.m. to 9 p.m. (closed Sun).

Specialty Stores & Markets

The Big Dipper, 1336 Oak Ave., St. Helena, CA 94574; (707) 963-2616. In business for 3 decades, the Big Dipper has an old-fashioned soda fountain ambience, and is one of the few places in this part of the Valley to get ice cream and milkshakes. Check out the daily hot lunch special, too. The store is on tree-lined Oak Avenue, a block west of and parallel to Main Street.

Dean & DeLuca, 607 St. Helena Hwy. (Hwy. 29), St. Helena, CA 94574; (707) 967-9980; www.deandeluca.com. Extensively remodeled in 2011, the only California location of the internationally renowned gourmet retailer features many locally made foods and fresh produce grown nearby. D&D's inventory is extensive, and it's all for preparing, serving, or eating food. In addition to rows of bottles and jars filled with sauces, tapenades, and olive oils, browse through the cheeses, dry pastas, Riedel and Vinum stemware and glassware, serving platters and bowls, and D&D logo aprons. Tea drinkers will love the huge selection of loose teas from around the world, and cookie and candy aficionados will be in nirvana. In the back is a deli cafe selling hot and cold sandwiches, grilled vegetables, salads, and grab-and-go items for picnics. Check out the Wine Hall, too, where all of the labels are from California producers.

Model Bakery, 1357 Main St. (Hwy. 29), St. Helena, CA 94574; (707) 963-8192; www.themodelbakery.com. For 75 years this site has been a bakery, and the historic brick ovens dating to the 1920s are still in use every day. As the only full-service bakery in St. Helena, Model Bakery's bread is served at many nearby restaurants and hotels, and also available in some stores. White and whole-wheat sourdough breads are their specialty, the loaves hand formed and made with organic flour, then coated with rice flour. Don't miss the English muffins (see the City of Napa chapter for the bakery's listing there), or any of their pastries. Besides baked goods, at least two sandwich options are offered daily, along with soup and salads, slices of brick-oven pizza, and other savory items for eating here at one of the eight tables, or taking away for a picnic. If you sit in the bakery long enough, you might see a celebrity walk in to score a sticky bun. Though Model Bakery has a second location in Napa, nearly all of the baking is done here.

Napa Valley Coffee Roasting Company, 1400 Oak Ave., St. Helena, CA 94574; (707) 963-4491; www .napavalleycoffee.com. See more about this coffee business and the Napa location in the City of Napa chapter. The St. Helena store is a block off Main Street on a quiet street corner, a big space full of natural light and with a few outdoor tables to watch St. Helenans going about their business. Up for a flavor challenge? Order the maple bacon latte.

Napa Valley Olive Oil Manufacturing Company, 835 Charter Oak Ave., St. Helena, CA 94574; (707) 963-4173; www.oliveoils ainthelena.com. Descriptors that apply here: a hidden gem, a treasure, unpretentious, functional, down to earth. In a plain white barn at the end of Charter Oak Avenue is perhaps the least elegant store in all of Napa Valley, and one of its best. Built in 1883, the barn was purchased by Guglielmo Guidi in the early 1940s. He converted it into an olive oil factory, and his two original olive presses are still on the property, though the oil is now pressed elsewhere. Inexpensive and available in small to bulk sizes, the oil's reputation among cooks is stellar. Owned by the same family since 1961, this Italian market is one of the finest for gathering authentic ingredients. They offer imported mushrooms by the pound, sweet peppers in jars, dry pastas of all types, dry beans in bulk for bagging yourself, herbs, cheese, Italian cookies, ropes of salami strung from the ceiling, and even their own line of soaps and lotions rich with olive oil. You'll want to linger here, as if it were an old general store where townsfolk gather to gossip and swap recipes. A few thousand business cards connected by small bits of tape hang everywhere like stalactites, with new visitors continually adding their calling cards. Outside are picnic tables for enjoying the goodies you purchased inside.

Napa Valley Vintage Home, 1201 Main St. (Hwy. 29), St. Helena, CA 94574; (707) 963-7423; www.napavalleyvintagehome .com. On the corner of Main and Spring Streets is this well-stocked home store with beautiful objects on display, but the serving pieces, cookbooks, and long French baguette boards really stand out. Founded by an interior designer, the focus of Vintage Home is not on cooking but how to present what you cook to your guests. Trays, placemats, stemware, tableware, ceramics, and kitchen and table linens from France and Italy are of superior quality, destined to become family heirlooms. Vintage Home is the type of store where your significant other waits outside while you bite your nails deciding which of the John Derian–designed decoupage letter plates you can't live without.

Olivier Napa Valley, 1375 Main St. (Hwy. 29), St. Helena, CA 94574; (707) 967-9777; www.oliviernapavalley.com. Many years ago I made the switch to olive oil in my kitchen with some hesitation, reluctant to leave behind the cheap corn oil I'd grown up using. After converting to EVOO (that's extra-virgin olive oil to the uninitiated), I had to be further educated on the differences between the types of olive oil that are best for high-heat sautéing, those most suited for "drizzling" onto food and for "finishing" a dish, how to use the flavored varieties, and so on. If you haven't yet switched from traditional corn or canola oil, a few minutes in this store will convince you to get your act together. Start by interacting with the do-it-yourself olive oil dispensers—push down on the knobs to try the different flavors, from mild to more pungent. Olivier's oils come from Spanish olive trees grown in California. This store also has a huge assortment of bottled and jarred ingredients bearing the Olivier Napa Valley label, such as sauces, marinades, flavored balsamic vinegars, dips, and dressings. Consider one of the attractive olivewood serving pieces, too, and pick up some gift items like olive oil soaps, dried lavender, and cookbooks.

St. Helena Olive Oil Company, 1351 Main St. (Hwy. 29), St. Helena, CA 94574; (800) 939-9880; www.sholiveoil.com. Once upon a time this building housed the Bank of Italy, complete with a cool vault in the back. Then it was a nightclub for many years. Now it's the downtown St. Helena location of this two-location business (the other store and the production facility is in Rutherford—see that chapter). Buy a jar of butternut squash pasta sauce—you won't regret it.

Spice Islands Marketplace, Culinary Institute of America at Greystone (CIA), 2555 Main St. (Hwy. 29), St. Helena, CA 94574; (707) 967-2309 or (888) 424-2433; www.ciachef.edu/California, or www.ciastore.com. The kitchen and gift store within the CIA was recently reconfigured to make room for a Flavor Bar (more about that below). But to call this a "kitchen" store doesn't do it justice. Sure, you can buy a whisk or a spatula, but if you are truly serious about mastering gourmet cooking as it is taught to the professional chefs within these massive stone walls, gather up some pots and pans, a few CIA cookbooks, and cool chef's apparel. Cookbooks in particular loom large here, with hundreds of titles stacked high on shelves. Ask about a particular food subject or cooking method and there's likely a book about it, some signed by the author. The Flavor Bar is where you can "taste like a chef" for only a few bucks. The sensory experiences include a "calibrate your palate" presentation to learn how chefs balance flavors just right. You can also taste super-premium olive oils and explore the alchemy behind chocolate (and peek into the adjacent chocolate laboratory through the window at the end of the bar). The Flavor Bar tastings take place two or three times daily ($10 to $15 per person), and reservations are encouraged, so check the website for the latest schedule.

Steves Housewares, 1370 Main St. (Hwy. 29), St. Helena, CA 94574; (707) 963-3423; www.stevessthelena.com. The housewares side of Steves sits next to the hardware store, with separate Main Street entrances but connected by a walkway inside. The hardware store came first, and has been an institution in this town for decades. The housewares annex is much newer, bursting with all manner of food preparation equipment for any type of cooking and baking. Select from cookie cutters in more than 100 fun shapes, Le Creuset and All-Clad cookware, bar and wine accessories, linens, teapots, cake decorating supplies, canning supplies, small appliances, and every sort of kitchen utensil under the sun. Don't fight for a parking spot on Main Street—go around to the back of the building.

Sunshine Foods, 1115 Main St. (Hwy. 29), St. Helena, CA 94574; (707) 963-7070; www.sunshinefoodsmarket.com. When you walk in, the deli is to the right and the cheese department is to the left. Those may be the areas of this store that interest you most, but the regular aisles are chock-full of interesting local products, so keep browsing. The produce department is outstanding, unique gifts are scattered around in special displays, and there's a fresh coffee stand, too. But it's the ready-made foods that bring in the faithful: six different kinds of soup, hot chicken to go, sushi, fresh bread from Bouchon Bakery, an olive bar, and a large selection of salads, sandwiches, and exceptional main-dish entrees. Strike up a conversation with James

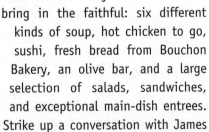

in the cheese department—a man whose knowledge of cheese is surpassed only by his love of talking about it.

Woodhouse Chocolate, 1367 Main St. (Hwy. 29), St. Helena, CA 94574; (800) 966-3468; www.woodhousechocolate.com. This is a chocolate shop tricked out like a high-end jewelry salon, à la Tiffany, where the sweet products under glass are given the same reverence as diamonds and sapphires. The clever window dressings, the chandelier, the tapestry on the wall, the elegant displays, and even the Tiffany-like blue packaging all spotlight the heavenly confections that are manufactured on the premises. Try a few truffles coated in cocoa powder, or the salty savory bars flavored with herbs and spices (chile and cumin with pink salt, for example). The founders of the store are wine-industry veterans who refocused their business skills into developing fine chocolates to rival those found in Europe, and they never looked back.

Farmers' Markets & Farm Stands

Dr. Dinwittie's Peaches, northwest corner of Deer Park Road and Silverado Trail, St. Helena, CA 94574. During the peach harvesting season, this basic covered farm stand at a four-way stop is buzzing with activity. Wendell Dinwittie is a retired orthopedic surgeon who owns the peach orchard here and rustles up the fruit for passers-by.

Several varieties are grown in this orchard so the fruits ripen over a succession of weeks, from early July to Labor Day—fresh from the tree, inexpensive, and delicious. Try to get to the stand before afternoon, or that day's harvest might already be sold out.

St. Helena Farmer's Market, Crane Park, Grayson Avenue near Crane Avenue, St. Helena, CA 94574; (707) 486-2662; www .sthelenafarmersmkt.org. On Friday morning from May through October, Crane Park becomes *the* place to be in St. Helena. Get there early for the best selection of fresh produce: the market opens at 7:30 a.m. and packs up at noon. Many of the food producers who appear at the market are described in this book: Long Meadow Ranch, Annie the Baker, Marshall's Farm Honey, Big Ranch Farm, La Saison, and others. A few vendors are from out of the area, or neighboring Sonoma County, but most are Napa Valley–based. Generally speaking you can buy vegetables, fruits, cheese, cookies, coffee and pastries, olive oil, nuts, handmade soaps, fresh flowers, and other good stuff. There's usually a chef's demonstration, too. Make this market a family affair—the kids will love the skateboard park and the shady playground and picnic area. Parking isn't a problem, and the restrooms are clean.

Goat's Leap Cheese, (707) 963-2337; www.goatsleap.com. Available only in limited quantities at certain times of the year, the cheese made by this small-production farm is highly prized and sought after by locals. The goats are the La Mancha breed, and the owners named the cheese varieties after some of their does: Sumi, Hyku, Kiku, and Carmela. The Kiku cheese is enhanced with Sauvignon Blanc wine and wrapped in fig leaves from trees grown on the owner's property; the Sumi is a flat-topped pyramid of outstanding flavor and texture. Cheese making at Goat's Leap is seasonal, so check with area stores such as Sunshine Foods in St. Helena and Cal Mart in Calistoga for availability.

Napa Valley Fudge Company, (707) 968-0870; www.napavalley fudge.com. A lifelong search for great fudge led to this family-run enterprise. With no culinary training and an occupation about as far removed from the kitchen as you can get (landfill manager), Gary Ponder has been fine-tuning his recipe for years. Gary was determined to make the type of fudge he liked—not what was available commercially. His bars are technically fudge but unlike any fudge you've sunk your teeth into before. There's no flour in the recipe, so the product is gluten-free. It's a simple mixture of dark and milk chocolates, butter, milk, marshmallow, and vanilla. (No nuts are added, but a future product might include nuts.) A creamy and not overtly sweet confection, the fudge is all made by hand. It's

THE CULINARY INSTITUTE
OF AMERICA AT GREYSTONE:
THE STORY BEHIND THE BUILDING

Before it was the Culinary Institute of America (CIA), the massive stone structure along Highway 29 north of St. Helena was called Greystone Cellars. Completed in 1889, it served as a cooperative winery for many of Napa Valley's early grape growers and was the largest stone winery in the world at that time for processing and storing wine (with a capacity of 2 million gallons). The building has 22-inch-thick walls of locally quarried tufa stone, and it covers a lot of real estate—117,000 square feet.

At the close of the 19th century and throughout Prohibition (1920 to 1933) and the Great Depression, Greystone sat mostly unused. The California Wine Association bought it for a song ($10,000) before the Christian Brothers, a Catholic teaching order, purchased the property in 1950 to produce their popular wines, brandies, and ports. Brother Timothy ran the show then, and his famous corkscrew collection— 1,000-plus items—is still on exhibit on the first floor. During this era, the building was added to the National Register of Historic Places.

Enter the mega corporation: In 1990, Heublein, Inc., an international distributor of food and beverages, acquired Greystone and the exclusive marketing rights to the Christian Brothers' brands. The deal was wrapped up just after the infamous Loma Prieta earthquake of 1989, which had damaged the northern section of the structure. Heublein then found a new buyer: the New York–based CIA. Once again, the building and the surrounding grounds, plus a nearby Merlot vineyard, were sold cheap, for 10 percent of its $14 million appraised value in 1993. The renovation and seismic retrofit took a couple of years to finish and cost more than $15 million. The Culinary Institute opened its doors in August 1995 for classes for food and wine professionals from around the world, and it's also been a popular stop ever since for food enthusiasts, diners, and culinary hobbyists.

When you walk through the restored redwood doors at the entrance, note how many of the building's historic features have been preserved, including some of the stills and special equipment that were used to make brandy. Wondering about those flags overhead in the 90-foot atrium? They represent the major wine-producing nations around the globe. One curiosity on display is a cornerstone set during the original construction in 1888. Inside were placed seven bottles of wine, a copy of the *St. Helena Star* from April 13, 1888, and foreign and rare coins ponied up by the workers. A hundred years later, four of the seven bottles were accidentally broken when workers attempted to replace the cornerstone with a time capsule.

Upstairs is the Vintners Hall of Fame, saluting many of the California wine industry's pioneers and current movers and shakers. The second floor is also the site of a small but fascinating display for any devoted oenophile: a 150-bottle collection of rare and influential wines.

Culinary Institute of America at Greystone (CIA)
2555 Main St. (Hwy. 29)
St. Helena, CA 94574
(707) 967-2320
www.ciachef.edu/california

available in half-pound and quarter-pound bars directly from the website, or in Napa Valley markets such as Vallerga's and Cal Mart, at the Napa General Store and Oakville Grocery, and the V. Sattui and Benessere wineries. If you happen to be waiting for a flight in the San Francisco airport's new Terminal 2, Gary's fudge is there, too, in the Napa Farms Market store. Gary's wife Beth and daughter Lauren comprise the trio that runs the company.

Panevino Food for Wine, (707) 963-2786; www.panevino-napa .com. Based in St. Helena, chefs David Katz and Mimi Katz are busy caterers who cooked up a great product a few years back: Panevino No. 6 Grissini. Better known as breadsticks, these grissini come in three flavors (sea salt, cheddar, and olive and herbs) and in two lengths, packaged in see-through cylinders. The slender, handmade sticks are baked in St. Helena (about 15,000 each week) and have a remarkable shelf life for a bread product (7 weeks). A package of the 15-inch breadsticks makes a dramatic table centerpiece for a wine tasting. In fact, the product was developed with wine tasting in mind, and the Katzes' grissini can be found in some of Napa Valley's finer wine tasting rooms for use as a palate refresher. The sticks are also stocked in stores such as Cal Mart in Calistoga, Ranch Market Too in Yountville, the Oxbow Cheese Merchant in the Oxbow Public Market in Napa, and Sunshine Foods in St. Helena.

Benessere Vineyards, 1010 Big Tree Rd., St. Helena, CA 94574; (707) 963-5853; www.benesserevineyards.com. **Benessere** is the Italian word for well-being. Many of us like to think that chocolate plays a role in well-being, and so the chocolate-and-wine tasting at this winery might be the answer to whatever ails you. It's best if you call ahead to arrange the type of tasting you desire, and the staff can probably oblige on short notice. Benessere is inspired by Italian wines, and so it bottles Sangiovese and Zinfandel primarily, but also Pinot Noir, Merlot, Syrah, a Sangiovese/Cabernet Sauvignon blend called Phenomenon, and a varietal called Aglianico, grown in limited quantities in California. Pinot Grigio is their white wine. A flight of five current wine releases is available for $15. Well off the busy Highway 29, Benessere is one of the smaller family-owned wineries in Napa Valley, and the attention you receive here is warm and friendly. Reservations for tastings and tours are required. Open daily from 10 a.m. to 5 p.m.; the last tasting takes place at 4:30 p.m. (A bit of trivia: The late, great tenor Luciano Pavarotti once made a film called *Yes, Giorgio* that was partially shot at this location.) See Certified Sommelier Eric G. Hensel's recipe for **Angel Hair with Clams, Chorizo, Saffron, Orange, Tomato & Cilantro** on p. 235.

Beringer Vineyards, 2000 Main St. (Hwy. 29), St. Helena, CA 94574; (866) 708-9463; www.beringer.com. **When I vacationed**

in wine country before moving here, Beringer was one of the first wineries I toured. Today it still proudly offers frequent tours as well as tastings. The Rhine House, the impressive mansion facing the highway, was completed in 1884 at a cost of $28,000, a fortune at the time. It was Frederick Beringer's house, a 17-room Victorian masterpiece with 40 panels of stained glass that harked back to his home in Germany. Today it's where you can taste the winery's reserve wines. The Beringer wine collection is extensive, ranging from inexpensive blush wines such as White Zinfandel to ultra-premium Cabernet Sauvignon, and about everything in between in red and white varietals. Tours and tastings take place daily approximately every 30 minutes between 11 a.m. and 4 p.m. The 30-minute introductory tour ($20 for adults, all ages welcome) takes visitors through the historic property's old stone winery and wine-aging tunnels, which were hand-chiseled more than a century ago by Chinese immigrants. For a bit more ($30 per person, 21 and over), the 60-minute tour includes a visit to the demonstration vineyard and ends with a tasting of four wines. In both cases, take note of the leaning oak (or "drunken" oak, as they once referred to it). Several other wine tasting options are offered, including the reserve tasting in the Rhine House, a tasting in the old winery, a retrospective of Beringer's private reserve Cabernet Sauvignon, and private tastings by appointment (with cheese plates available). Beringer is located at the south end of the stands of elm trees that line both sides of the highway. It's open daily from 10 a.m. to 6 p.m.

Charles Krug Winery, 2800 Main St. (Hwy. 29), St. Helena, CA 94574; (707) 967-2229; www.charleskrug.com. This winery takes the prize for being the "oldest" in Napa Valley, founded in 1861. Many of the Valley's first wine pioneers were from other countries, and Charles Krug was from Prussia. The winery came under new ownership about 30 years later when Charles died, but the name stuck for historic reasons. Prohibition put an end to wine production here, but during World War II it started up again with new owners, the Mondavi family, who continue to run the business, and Peter Mondavi Sr. still overseeing operations. The Charles Krug name is synonymous with red Bordeaux varietals, especially Cabernet Sauvignon. Other reds include Pinot Noir, Zinfandel, and Merlot. The Charles Krug white varietals are Chardonnay and Sauvignon Blanc. On Saturday at 2 p.m., the winery conducts a barrel tasting to match its limited-release and family-reserve wines with artisanal cheeses. Lasting approximately 90 minutes and costing $50 per person, the tasting is limited to eight participants. (During the busier summer season, the barrel tasting may also be offered on Friday.) Reservations are required for the barrel tasting, which takes place in the winery's redwood cellar, built in 1882 and recently renovated. The winery's public tasting room is open daily for wine-only tasting from 10:30 a.m. to 5 p.m.

Clif Family Winery at Velo Vino, 709 Main St. (Hwy. 29), St. Helena, CA 94574; (707) 968-0625; www.cliffamilywinery.com. If you love Clif Bars, don't miss this tasting room. The founders and CEOs of the Clif Bar empire, makers of all-natural and organic energy foods and drinks, are also cycling enthusiasts and wine producers. So the idea of pairing bike riding and wine tasting seemed a natural. Park your two wheels outside and then sip the Clif label Sauvignon Blanc, Petite Sirah, Zinfandel, or Cabernet Sauvignon while munching on new Clif Bar flavors. The tasting room sells and offers tastes of other Clif products, such as olive oils, Luna bars, and trail mixes in several flavor combinations. A private food-and-wine tasting is also available ($25 per person), with prior reservations. Velo Vino also arranges custom bike tours—call the tasting room for more information. Open daily from 10 a.m. to 6 p.m.

Del Dotto Vineyards, 1445 St. Helena Hwy. (Hwy. 29), St. Helena, CA 94574; (707) 963-2134; www.deldottovineyards.com. Two ginormous terra-cotta urns mark the entrance to this winery on Highway 29. Inside, the decor is dripping with Old World elegance, from the acres of Italian marble to the sprinkling of Venetian chandeliers, and the aging caves are also decorated to reflect the Del Dotto family's Italian heritage. Del Dotto produces Cabernet Sauvignon, Merlot, Cabernet Franc, Sangiovese, and Pinot Noir, and by the time you read this they might also have a Chardonnay on the market. The in-house chef creates one of the wine-and-food pairings—what they call the Estate Cave Experience and Wine Tasting. You go into the cave for a barrel tasting of several different varietals, then return to the main tasting hall for more wine matched with meats and cheeses, and finished with a chocolate-and-port pairing. Lasting about an hour and offered several times daily, the cave tasting is $50 per person. Less expensive is the Estate Winery

Bar Tasting ($30), with a sampling of cheeses matched to four wines and a port. Almonds and handmade dark chocolate round out the experience. Reservations are required for both tastings. The winery is open daily from 11 a.m. to 5 p.m.

Flora Springs Winery, 677 St. Helena Hwy. (Hwy. 29), St. Helena, CA 94574 (The Room); (707) 967-8032 or (866) 967-8032; and 1978 W. Zinfandel Ln., St. Helena, CA 94574; (707) 967-6723 (The Estate); www.florasprings.com. Wine-and-food pairings take place in two locations—the tasting room on the highway called the Room, next door to Dean & DeLuca, and the site of the winery's caves, called the Estate, farther south and off the highway. The Komes and Garvey families have operated this winery for more than 30 years, when they took what was once a long-neglected "ghost" winery built in the mid-1880s and brought it back to productive use. Flora Springs bottles many varietals, including Cabernet Sauvignon, Pinot Grigio, Sangiovese, Merlot, Chardonnay, and Sauvignon Blanc. Tastings with food at the Room are varied (call for pricing), from a Taste of Asia to a Taste of France. The fare can range from cheese and chocolate to Mediterranean and Asian-inspired nibbles. The Vineyard Courtyard Picnic option ($45 per person) includes three wines and the basics you need for a picnic (linens, glassware, etc.). The Library Tasting and Tour at the Estate ($55 per person) is a 90-minute guided look around the property that ends with a pairing of several well-aged wines (up to 15 years old) with small plates of food prepared by the in-house chef. Advance reservations are required for the food-paired tastings and tours. The Room is open daily from 10:30 a.m. to 5 p.m.; the Estate is open for tours and tasting by appointment only.

Hall Winery, 401 St. Helena Hwy. (Hwy. 29), St. Helena, CA 94574; (707) 967-2626 or (866) 667-4255; www.hallwines.com. Hall places a lot of emphasis on pairing wine with food, and they host at least one big annual event to call attention to that fact and share the fun. Drop-in tasters are always welcome for wine tasting only, but the wine-and-cheese pairing with a tour of the production facility is available once daily at 11 a.m. Mon through Fri ($45 per person, reservations required). On weekends, once each day at 11 a.m., the food-and-wine experience is enhanced ($75 per person). It includes the tour of the facility plus what I would call "lunch"—an amuse bouche (a small dollop of something good), followed by summer vegetables with curry and coconut, pork tenderloin with chickpeas, beef with red onion marmalade, and a cheese course to finish. Along with that are five tastes of Hall wines, from their Sauvignon Blancs to Cabernet Sauvignons. Hall also makes a Merlot, a Cabernet Franc, and some blended reds. The tasting room is open daily from 10 a.m. to 5:30 p.m. The food-focused annual event is their Cabernet Cook-Off, held on a Saturday afternoon in late April or early May. Teams of chefs, some amateur and some professional, compete to win money for their favorite Napa Valley nonprofit organizations. The chefs whip up the dishes to pair with Hall's Cabernet, the attendees enjoy the grub, and a panel of judges from the food and wine industry vote on the winners. Everyone walks away well fed and happy. It's inexpensive, too—$55 per person.

Long Meadow Ranch Winery, 738 Main St. (Hwy. 29), St. Helena, CA 94574; (707) 963-4555; www.longmeadowranch.com. It's difficult to imagine that the white Gothic farmhouse at this site, built in 1874 and known as the Logan-Ives House, was uninhabitable until 2009. That's when Long Meadow Ranch (LMR) set about rebuilding and renovating the buildings at this former nursery property for other uses. The farmhouse is beautiful and inviting now, the perfect environment for tasting LMR's superior wines and extra virgin olive oils. The wines (Cabernet Sauvignon, Sangiovese, a tasty blend called Ranch House Red, and Sauvignon Blanc) are all made from certified organic grapes, reflecting the Hall family's socially responsible mission of using sustainable farming methods. No appointment is necessary for wine and olive oil tasting, but reservations are required for the wine-and-food experiences. That includes the Logan-Ives House Pairing ($55 per person), matching LMR's Sauvignon Blanc with, perhaps, house-made mortadella and a salad, followed by the Cabernet Sauvignon with oak-grilled chicken and flageolet beans, kale, and *salsa verde*. The Farm-to-Table Experience ($85 per person) is three courses paired with three LMR wines (example: shaved asparagus salad with grass-fed beef terrine, roasted pork, and buttermilk panna cotta with samples of Sauvignon Blanc and two Cabernet Sauvignons). For the complete

LMR experience, book the Napa Valley Dream ($150 per person—once daily), a 3-hour odyssey that begins at the Logan-Ives House with pastry, fruit, and coffee. You're then driven to the 650-acre Hall family ranch to see the winery, olive oil pressing facility, caves, vineyards, and olive orchards. Back at the Logan-Ives House, you're treated to food-and-wine pairings similar to the Farm-to-Table experience. The tasting room is open daily from 11 a.m. to 6 p.m. (See Foodie Faves for information about **Farmstead Restaurant,** also at this location.)

Merryvale Vineyards, 1000 Main St. (Hwy. 29), St. Helena, CA 94574; (707) 963-7777, (707) 968-3425 or (888) 963-0576; www .merryvale.com. It's easy to walk to Merryvale if you happen to be window-shopping around downtown St. Helena anyway. Find it south of the stoplight and across from Gott's Roadside drive-in. The historic winery was the first to be built in Napa Valley following Prohibition, and the Merryvale brand was established here in 1983. The winery produces Cabernet Sauvignon, Merlot, Chardonnay, Sauvignon Blanc, Pinot Noir, and others. Sign on for the wine-and-cheese pairing ($45 per person) on Friday and Saturday, when the staff wine specialist and sommelier selects artisanal cheese and a selection of charcuterie to pair with five tastes of Merryvale's red and white elixirs (reservations required). Four times a year, the winery conducts a barrel tasting event ($25 per person), featuring samples of food and tastes of their wines "thieved" directly from the barrels, where they are still being aged. Live entertainment is provided, too, and reservations are not required. Merryvale is open daily from 10 a.m. to 6:30 p.m.

Newton Vineyard, 2555 Madrona Ave., St. Helena, CA 94574; (707) 963-9000; www.newtonvineyard.com. For the gardens alone, Newton is worth seeking out. (And underneath the ornamental garden is a wine aging cave.) The view is stunning, too, from this property in the Spring Mountain grape-growing AVA, or appellation. Newton conducts a wine tasting together with small bites of food twice daily, Tues through Sun ($40 per person). The pairings might be poached pears and marcona almonds with Chardonnay, a chocolate-lavender truffle with Merlot, and smoked sausage and huckleberries with Cabernet Sauvignon. There are many Bordeaux-style blends bottled in Napa Valley, but my vote for the best blend name is "The Puzzle," Newton's cherry and plummy mixture of Cabernet Sauvignon, Merlot, Petit Verdot, and Cabernet Franc. They also bottle unfiltered Chardonnay, Merlot, and Cabernet Sauvignon. (It's technical, but "unfiltered" generally means that more of the raw grape solids are left in the bottom of the barrel during aging to enhance flavor, then the clean wine is decanted out of the barrel from the top and placed in bottles without filtration.) Newton is open by appointment only for tours and tastings, so call ahead to arrange your visit.

Raymond Vineyards, 849 Zinfandel Ln., St. Helena, CA 94574; (707) 963-3141 or (707) 963-2945; www.raymondvineyards.com. Once owned by the Japanese brewing giant Kirin, Raymond Vineyards is now back to being a "family-owned" business, operated by Boisset Family Estates, which oversees several boutique wineries in California. With new ownership came a larger tasting room, remodeled to include, among other new features, an insectary that demonstrates the importance of the winery's organic and biody-namic farming methods. Science aside, the food-and-wine pairings have been expanded too. A four-cheese and four-wine tasting ($25 per person) is offered in the barrel room, "without the usual infor-mation overload," says a tasting room pourer. A component tasting ($40 per person) includes multiple food samples with the wine. More class-like sessions are also available, going in-depth into the art of blending wine ($35) and the art of aerating and decanting wine ($30). These tastings and classes are held weekdays beginning at 12:30 p.m., and require advance reservations. Raymond bottles many varietals, but Cabernet Sauvignon is their signature wine. Also bearing Raymond labels are Zinfandel, Petite Sirah, Chardonnay, a meritage blend, and proprietary red and white blends. Open 10 a.m. to 4 p.m. daily.

Sutter Home Family Vineyards, 277 St. Helena Hwy. (Hwy. 29), St. Helena, CA 94574; (707) 963-3104; www.sutterhome.com. Sutter Home is the Trinchero family's most widely known label and its least expensive wines (see the following listing for more about the family's history and its ultra-premium line of wines). The

Trincheros developed and aggressively marketed White Zinfandel in the 1970s and 1980s on the Sutter Home label, and for years afterward there was a lot of eye-rolling among wine purists. But, honestly, many people not in the wine industry (and that's most people) started on the path to drinking really good wines after consuming gallons of Sutter Home's soda-poppy White Zin. It convinced them to explore wine in-depth and eventually move up to the classic varietals made from ultra-premium wine grapes. So, while the naysayers think White Zin was a step backward for the Napa Valley wine industry, I believe it nudged the other wineries ever forward to produce more and better wines, thereby introducing casual wine drinkers to higher quality products. Because isn't that the goal of the industry—to convince consumers to enjoy wine as an everyday beverage with food, and not just on special occasions? With White Zin, Sutter Home made wine drinking inexpensive and easy, and it really does go well with certain foods. It's also refreshing on a hot summer day. That said, you can taste today's White Zin at the Sutter Home tasting room along with several other varietals that bear the Sutter Home label, most of which are produced from less expensive grapes not grown in Napa Valley. That beautiful Victorian mansion you see on the property is not the tasting room—it's a private inn for invited guests only. But you are welcome to walk through the lovely gardens there. The visitors' center, where the tasting takes place, is housed in the property's original winery building.

The hours are 10 a.m. to 5 p.m. daily, and much of the tasting is complimentary.

Trinchero Napa Valley Winery, 3070 St. Helena Hwy. (Hwy. 29), St. Helena, CA 94574; (707) 963-1160; www.trincheronapa valley.com. Pronounced with a hard "c" and silent "h," the winery bearing the family name is a producer of excellent Cabernet Sauvignon, Merlot, a meritage blend, Sauvignon Blanc, and others. The Trinchero legacy in Napa Valley goes back to 1948, when Mario and Mary Trinchero moved from New York City to the Valley and bought a 19th-century winery called **Sutter Home** (see above) that had been abandoned. The business started small, but the world began to take notice when Bob Trinchero, Mary and Mario's son, created the first White Zinfandel wine in 1972. Years later, flush with success and cash, the Trincheros started buying vineyards in the Valley and now own more than 200 acres of prime grapes. The winery at this location is their luxury property, where the higher-end wines they produce from Napa Valley grapes are tasted. The buildings are nearly new and include the winery, an extensive hospitality center, and the tasting room. Two tasting seminars are offered: a Taste of Terroir ($40 per person) for understanding how a vineyard's physical site impacts the wine in the glass, and the Sensory Challenge for using your senses to identify the aromas in wine ($35). Seminars are conducted three times daily by appointment only. Several other respected labels are part of the Trinchero family of wines, including Napa Valley's Folie à Deux.

V. Sattui Winery, 1111 White Ln., St. Helena, CA 94574; (707) 963-7774 or (800) 799-2337; www.vsattui.com. The nearest thing to a Disney-like experience in Napa Valley may be V. Sattui. Owner Dario Sattui renovated this winery in 1985 with the intention of turning it into a "village" setting. (He's also the man responsible for the grandiose "kingdom" he calls **Castello di Amorosa,** another Disney-ish experience south of Calistoga—see that chapter.) The setting in St. Helena is lovely, with old oaks, old buildings, and lots of picnic tables, but it does attract visitors by the busload. So if you don't like being jostled while gazing at cheese, T-shirts, cork-screws, and cookbooks, concentrate instead on the wine. Many of V. Sattui's varietals are medal winners, so the quality is pretty good and a tasting might be worth your time and effort. The deli is com-prehensive, too, with plenty of hot and cold entrees and salads, and everything else you need for an elegant picnic. In 2011, V. Sattui began food-and-wine pairings (Mon through Thurs from 11 a.m. to 3 p.m., Apr through Oct), with several options available. For instance, one tasting features Sauvignon Blanc with Italian seafood salad, a Semillon with pecorino, and a Dry Riesling with Thai noodles. The pairings are affordable ($19 per person) and reserva-tions are not necessary. If you like the combinations you try, all of the foods are for sale in the deli, so you can re-create the tasting experience at home. V. Sattui sells about 40 different wines at any time, and they are only for sale at the winery, online, or by mail. Drop in to taste the wines any day of the week from 9 a.m. to 6 p.m.—no appointment required.

Silverado Brewing Company, 3020 St. Helena Hwy. (Hwy. 29), St. Helena, CA 94574; (707) 967-9876; www.silveradobrewing company.com. Forget for a moment that you're in Napa Valley, the world's playground for wine culture. You're craving a beer, a really good beer, and there's nothing wrong with that. A couple of miles north of St. Helena is Silverado Brewing Company, housed in what once was a winery·100 years ago (like so many old stone buildings in these parts), and converted in 2000 for making hand-crafted brews. It's also a good restaurant, so consider pairing your suds with sustenance. Did I mention the beer is fresh? So fresh it travels no more than 50 feet from the brewery to the glass in your hand. Try the Blonde Ale, a golden ale made from certified organic malts, with the calamari; or the Pale Ale matched with a salad or the flatiron steak. The Amber will wash down well with barbecued ribs, while the oatmeal stout is ideal for pairing with beef or chocolate. The restaurant promotes healthful and sustainable ingredients, local produce, zero trans fats in its fried foods, and so on. There's much to choose from on the menu—standard publike appetizers, a good selection of main-course salads, big plates from fish to ribs, pasta options, and sandwiches and burgers ($$). There's lots of parking, a beer garden, tap room, dining room, and friendly staff, too. Silverado opens daily at 11:30 a.m., and food is served until approximately 8:30 or 9 p.m., depending on how busy they get. The tap room stays open "as long as there are still people to serve," according to the barkeep.

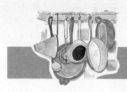

Learn to Cook

Culinary Institute of America at Greystone (CIA), 2555 Main St. (Hwy. 29), St. Helena, CA 94574; (707) 967-2320; www .ciachef.edu/california. CIA at Greystone is the West Coast outpost of America's most respected culinary school. If you're serious about furthering your chef skills or wine education, it doesn't get any more professional than the CIA. For visiting hobbyists and food enthusiasts, there are many opportunities to increase your knowledge of food and cooking. Some are short courses for a couple of hours or an afternoon, and others are weeklong "boot camps" that cover the fundamentals of cooking. The topics are wide ranging, from cake decorating to grilling, or learning the secrets of preparing Greek or Latin cuisine. For those working in the food industry, the curriculum for professionals is varied, with custom courses and hands-on classes in cooking, baking, pastry, management, and wine. Students can earn ProChef Certification on three different levels, and professional wine certification, too. The wine program in particular is extensive at CIA Greystone, covering everything from winemaking basics, to wine-and-food pairings, to the business of wine. All instructors are professional chefs, sommeliers, winemakers, and business consultants. Perhaps all you want to do is sit and watch while someone else does the cooking. Chef's demonstrations take place on weekends in the CIA's DeBaun Theatre, lasting about an hour and costing only $20 per person. Reservations are necessary for all food enthusiast classes and the demos. Check the CIA's website for updates. See Chef Sandy Dominguez's recipe for **Orzo & Green Bean Salad with Cucumbers, Apples & Parsley Vinaigrette** on p. 237.

Napa Valley College Cooking School, 1088 College Ave., St. Helena, CA 94574; (707) 967-2900 or (707) 967-2930; www.napa valley.edu/cookingschool. In a lovely setting just off Silverado Trail, this Upvalley branch of Napa Valley College is exclusively about food, and it's popular with locals and area chefs who want to sharpen their cooking skills in particular ways. It's also a straight-forward cooking school with a 14-month, 2-semester curriculum for budding new chefs. The school even has its own flock of egg-laying chickens. Classes for food and wine enthusiasts are generally more affordable than at the Culinary Institute (see previous listing), and are typically 3-hour evening or Saturday sessions led by local chefs or the school's executive chef, Barbara Alexander. Some of the classes offered in the school's most recent catalog included instruction in knife skills and maintenance, preparing Vietnamese cuisine, cooking fish, cheese making, mastering perfect pies, and even an in-depth class on brewing beer at home.

Calistoga

Visitors enjoy Calistoga for its compactness and accessibility. Like Yountville, Calistoga is largely walkable. Quirky, offbeat, and informal are other words that come to mind. There's plenty of good food in this little town, too, and one of Napa Valley's four seasonal farmers' markets unfolds on Saturday mornings near the pretty police station on Washington Street.

Generally speaking, Calistoga is more laid-back and affordable than other parts of the Valley. It's my favorite Valley town, and the nearest to my home. When I make the short drive to Calistoga, I leave behind my daily duties to wander to and fro on Lincoln Avenue and see what's new. I sink my teeth into a burger or a hearty breakfast, order a take-away gelato, and return to the sidewalk to admire how the window displays have changed with the seasons and the holidays.

When Sam Brannan founded the town in the mid-1800s, natural hot springs were bubbling up all over the place. He bought one square mile of land and set out to construct a super spa resort to appeal to San Francisco's wealthy upper class. It's widely believed

Sam was inebriated when he blurted out his intention to name the new acquisition "Calistoga." What he apparently tried to say was, "I'll make this place the Saratoga of California," because of his affection for another town full of hot water, Saratoga Springs, New York. But what came out was: "I'll make this place the Calistoga of Sarafornia." The inventive name caught on, and a tourist destination was born.

A short time later, the discovery of silver brought fortune hunters to Calistoga. Prosperity was brisk and robust, but didn't last long. When the silver vein was tapped out, the miners moved on. Yet the visitors who loved the hot, steamy water kept coming.

Today's vacationers in Calistoga come for affordable, basic spa experiences, as well as gooey but rejuvenating mud baths. They also discover that dining is less expensive than in the cities and towns farther down the highway.

Landmark Eateries

All Seasons Bistro, 1400 Lincoln Ave., Calistoga, CA 94515; (707) 942-9111; www.allseasonsnapavalley.net; $$. All Seasons is considered one of the first gourmet restaurants to open in Napa Valley, dating to the early 1980s, so I have to give it credit for longevity—something many good restaurants have not been able to achieve. It's a wine bar and wine shop, too, offering a long list of labels from around the world. Start the meal with lobster bisque or ahi tuna tartare, followed by seared duck breast with asparagus, black rice, and white mushrooms. The sun-filled cafe is at the corner of Lincoln Avenue and Washington Street. Its black-and-white checkerboard floor and red ceiling give it a European feel, like a bistro you might find in Paris. The owners can also cater your special event; ask for Alex or Gayle. Open for lunch and dinner, Tues through Sun. See Chef Summer Sebastiani's recipe for **Asparagus Soup with Mustard Greens and Cheddar/Mustard-Seed Crackers** on p. 219.

Brannan's Grill, 1374 Lincoln Ave., Calistoga, CA 94515; (707) 942-2233; www.brannansgrill.com; $$$. I like restaurants with staying power, and Brannan's is on that list. It opened in 1998, and is still one of the best places in the vicinity to have a good meal and a decent martini. Take note of the 27-foot mahogany bar, shipped around Cape Horn more than a century ago. They call the food here "new American" or "American style," with meat and fresh produce from local suppliers. That might include greens grown by Forni Brown Welsh Gardens, only a few blocks away. Brannan's menu sticks with classics such as king salmon, seared California sea bass, a double-cut pork chop, roasted chicken, hanger steak, and steak frites. Sides are extra and include risotto, macaroni and cheese, broccolini, and mashed potatoes. During warm weather, the windows open wide to reveal the sidewalk's human parade. It's almost alfresco, but more interesting. Live soft music is featured some nights. Open daily for lunch and dinner.

JoLé Farm to Table, 1457 Lincoln Ave., Calistoga, CA 94515; (707) 942-5938; www.jolerestaurant.com; $$$. The husband-and-wife chef team of Matt and Sonjia Spector owned their first restaurant in Philadelphia. JoLé is their second enterprise, offering small plates, or tasting menus of 4, 5, or 6 courses. The small plates might be veal sweetbreads with green-onion corn cakes in a dried-cherry and port reduction, or king salmon sashimi, or perhaps scallops with leeks and pancetta, a chicken-fried quail with a Cobb salad, or kale stew with ham and black-eyed peas. Save room for dessert—pastry chef Sonjia creates phenomenal sweets, such as key lime tart and frozen honey and red walnut nougat. There's house-made ice cream, too, and a great selection of international and California port. The coffee is from Calistoga's Yo el Rey Roasting. Located inside the Mount View Hotel, JoLé is open daily for dinner at 5 p.m.

Solbar at Solage Hotel, 755 Silverado Trail, Calistoga, CA 94515; (707) 226-0850; www.solbarnv.com; $$$. Solbar, the restaurant in the Solage hotel complex southeast of downtown Calistoga, is now the proud recipient of a Michelin star—Calistoga's first. That's atypical for a hotel restaurant, but it's really a spa resort, in keeping with the prevailing lodgings in this town. Therefore, the dinner menu at Solbar tends to straddle the fence: hearty cuisine without regard for calories (grilled loin of lamb or beef short ribs) balanced by more healthful and lighter fare (chilled crab or asparagus with salmon). If you're lucky, Lucky Pig will be served on the day you drive in: it's slow-roasted shoulder of pork with black-sesame crepes, pickled pineapple, Mongolian peanuts, lettuce cups and more—a meal for two. Anything on the menu can be enjoyed in the dining room, in the bar, or on the poolside patio, which seats 85. If your dog is riding along, he's welcome too, on the patio. Solbar has the feel of a southern California resort—look for the two large palm trees that bookend the entrance off Silverado Trail. Solbar is open to the public daily for breakfast (ask about the doughnuts), lunch (shrimp wraps or sliders), and dinner.

Foodie Faves

Barolo, 1457 Lincoln Ave., Calistoga, CA 94515; (707) 942-9900; www.barolocalistoga.com; $$. Located in the Mount View Hotel, this restaurant and wine tasting bar (previously called BarVino) is one of the newer spots in town, emphasizing contemporary Italian dishes, and with the contemporary red, black, and silver decor to match. I especially like the vintage red scooter up on the wall. On the menu are starters such as truffle fries, mussels, an antipasto platter, and artisanal cheese platter. Pizza is also available, along with minestrone and chilled gazpacho. Four or five pasta plates (in two sizes) and other entrees elevate Barolo from a simple wine tasting bar. The bartender also slings cocktails, so happy hour draws in the sidewalk strollers for the $1 mixed drinks and $5 glasses of wine. Open daily at 4:30 p.m. for dinner.

Bosko's Trattoria, 1364 Lincoln Ave., Calistoga, CA 94515; (707) 942-9088; www.boskos.com; $$. Serving Italian comfort food, this restaurant is housed in a building that dates to 1888, made from sandstone quarried on the Silverado Trail. You will see this same stone throughout Napa Valley in many buildings and bridges. There's still evidence of charred wood on the ceiling from a fire that ravaged the structure more than a century ago. Bosko's serves all those dishes you've come to expect at a good Italian trattoria: capocollo and sausage sandwiches, Napolitano-style pizza pulled from a wood-fired oven, minestrone, pancetta-wrapped meatloaf, and gnocchi. All of the pasta is made fresh daily on the premises. Finish the meal with tiramisu, or try the gelato soaked in espresso. A good selection of after-dinner port is available, too. Open daily for lunch and dinner.

Buster's Southern BBQ & Bakery, 1207 Foothill Blvd., Calistoga, CA 94515; (707) 942-5605; www.busterssouthernbbq .com; $. Barbecue joints are few and far between in Napa Valley, and that explains the popularity of Buster's, where Highway 29 meets Foothill Boulevard, at the flashing red stoplight. You might see—and smell—the smoke from the grills before you notice the building. Pork ribs, tri-tip, half-chickens, and hot links are always over the fire, for pairing with the traditional fixins of beans, potato salad, and coleslaw. Whole tri-tips, whole chickens, and racks of

ribs are available for take-
out so you can pretend you
did all the hard work your-
self. Buster's is also a soda
fountain, with shakes and
malts, cups and cones, floats
and freezes. Coffee is brewed, too,
at whatever strength of caffeine you need, from espresso to an
Americano. The "bakery" in the name refers to sweet-potato pies,
cookies, and muffins. Beer and wine are also poured. There's plenty
of parking and outdoor seating, too. Open daily from 9 a.m. until 8
p.m. (Sun 10 a.m. to 6 p.m.)

Cafe Sarafornia, 1413 Lincoln Ave., Calistoga, CA 94515; (707)
942-0555; www.cafesarafornia.com; $. Taking its name from Sam
Brannan's slip of the tongue (see the introduction to this chapter),
Sarafornia dishes up breakfast platters all day and lunch entrees,
too. Choose from several outstanding Benedicts, or the always-
satisfying huevos rancheros. For lunch, try to get your fork around
the giant Cobb Tower salad, or your mouth around the ⅓-pound
beef or turkey burger. Beer, wine, and mimosas are served, as well
as Muddy Marys—Bloody Mary mix with a beer. Look for the cafe's
dark green awning and red door. Open daily from 7 a.m. to 2:30 p.m.

Checker's, 1414 Lincoln Ave., Calistoga, CA 94515; (707) 942-
9300; www.checkerscalistoga.com; $. Shades of terra-cotta and the
oversized European posters give Checker's a warm, welcoming feel.

The Thai noodle salad is one of my favorites, but all of the salads are exceptional. Checker's also creates great soup. In fact, the restaurant earned the local Soup-er-Bowl award in 2009 for dishing up the best soup in town. The basket of bread delivered to your table with olive oil and balsamic vinegar sets the stage for the whole meal. It's difficult to categorize the food at Checker's, which also has a location in nearby Santa Rosa. Pizza, calzones, and pasta give it an Italian spin. Asian influences are sprinkled here and there in some of the dishes, and New Orleans pan-fried chicken is a nod to the South. The menu is multicultural and it's all good. For the best people-watching experience, ask for one of the round tables in the front windows. Open for lunch and dinner daily.

Flatiron Grill, 1440 Lincoln Ave., Calistoga, CA 94515; (707) 942-1220; www.flatirongrill.com; $$. Beef is the theme of the decor, starting with the sign of the bovine swinging in the breeze outside. So beef is what's on the menu. The house specialty—no surprise—is the flatiron steak, served with a confit of new potatoes, asparagus, and red-wine sauce. Yet there's something for everyone: fried chicken, stuffed trout, blackened catfish, and inventive salads (fried chicken appears again in an entrée-size salad). Maybe you desire a pulled-pork or portobello mushroom sandwich, or a hefty hamburger. Add a couple of sides, including hush puppies, if you're still hungry. Another plus: no corkage fee ("never, ever," the owners emphasize) when you bring in your own bottle of wine. That's a rarity in these parts. Open for dinner daily at 4:30 p.m.

Home Plate Cafe, 2448 Foothill Blvd., Calistoga, CA 94515; (707) 942-5646; www.maryshomeplate.com; $. If it's simple burgers and ice cream you desire, Home Plate knocks it out of the park. North of the main part of town, Home Plate is in the small retail center where Foothill Boulevard meets Petrified Forest Road. (Yes, there's a genuine petrified forest only a few miles from here.) Because of its location at a busy four-way stop, most people discover Home Plate on their way to somewhere else, intrigued by the banners that shout JUICY BURGERS and ICE CREAM PARLOR. It also appeals to locals for its affordable prices and quick service, so working stiffs like UPS drivers know all about it. For variety, the menu also includes chicken dinners, steak dinners, and hot and cold sandwiches. The 14 flavors of ice cream are available in cones or shakes. Order your food, claim a table outside, and watch the traffic parade going past—it's mesmerizing. Open daily at 7 a.m. for breakfast (except Wed, when it opens at 11), and from 8 a.m. to 8 p.m. weekends.

Hydro Bar & Grill, 1403 Lincoln Ave., Calistoga, CA 94515; (707) 942-9777; $$. It's small, and can get a little rowdy after a certain hour of the night, but that's part of the charm. I've had many good meals here—breakfast, lunch, and dinner. The burgers are always reliable, made of beef, turkey, or fish. Other specialties, which change with the fresh ingredients available, might be seared scallops, a cornmeal-dusted chile relleno, or grilled steak frites. In the mood to dance? This is usually the only place in Calistoga

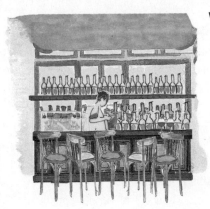

with rocking live music on weekend nights (by such great local bands as Hot Karma), so the sidewalk can get congested with party-seekers wanting to squeeze in. Hydro is a full bar, but you could also sit here all night trying to choose a beer from the large selection of imported suds and microbrews on tap. Because of Hydro's centralized location, the walks are short to most of the spa hotels, particularly if you've had too much, uh, fun. Open daily from 9 a.m. to midnight (to 1 a.m. on weekends).

Pacifico Restaurante Mexicano, 1237 Lincoln Ave., Calistoga, CA 94515; (707) 942-4400; www.pacificorestaurantemexicano.com; $$. Cue the mariachi band—Pacifico has live music most Friday nights. All of the reliable favorites of a good Mexican restaurant are on the menu, and the atmosphere is colorful and lively. There are plenty of appetizers and salads, including a vegetarian taco salad, plus burrito and fajita platters. Pacifico spotlights prawns in several ways (including a bacon- and pineapple-wrapped entrée), and 14 traditional-style combos, from *carne asada* to *mole poblano*. For lighter fare, stop in at happy hour for $4 quesadillas washed down with $4 margaritas. Outside patio dining is offered, too. Open weekdays 11 a.m. until 9 p.m. (weekends at 10 a.m. for breakfast).

Palisades Deli, 1458 Lincoln Ave., Calistoga, CA 94515; (707) 942-0145; www.palisadescafe.com; $. Always on the lookout for famous faces, I said "hello" here once to Wavy Gravy of Woodstock fame (he's also a respected Bay Area activist and colorful character). He was pigging out by himself on something delicious, judging by the thumbs-up he gestured in my direction, because his mouth was too full to speak. The deli is inside Calistoga's old train depot, which has seen better times. Many of the shops in the building and the refurbished rail cars outside have come and gone too frequently, but this deli seems to be prospering regardless. There's seating inside and out, and lots to pick from on the menu: cold sandwiches, hot sandwiches (try the Hot Valley Veggie), two kinds of wraps, burritos, tacos, and 10 different side salads. For early risers, breakfast sandwiches are offered, along with an espresso bar. Open daily from 7 a.m. to 6 p.m.

Puerto Vallarta Mexican Restaurant, 1473 Lincoln Ave., Calistoga, CA 94515; (707) 942-6563; $. It's easy to walk right past this eatery, with the entrance behind the Scoops & Swirls ice cream shop, but it's worth finding. Outdoor seating is limited, but the inside dining room is spacious and inviting. Most of the menu represents traditional Mexican specialties: tacos, burritos, enchiladas, fajitas. Shake up your taste buds with the Campechana Vallarta, a shrimp and octopus cocktail brimming with tomatoes, onions, cilantro, and avocado. Mexican beer and sodas, house red and white wines, and margaritas are served, too. Open 11 a.m. to 8:30 p.m. Mon through Fri; 10 a.m. to 8 p.m. weekends.

Soo Yuan, 1354 Lincoln Ave., Calistoga, CA 94515; (707) 942-9404; $. As the only Chinese restaurant around for miles, Soo Yuan is your source for lemon chicken or moo shu pork when the craving strikes. The most expensive item on the menu is Seafood in a Bird Nest ($14.50), so it's also one of the best bargains in the vicinity. Specializing in Mandarin and Szechuan cuisine, Soo Yuan can be counted on for the usual beef, chicken, pork, and seafood dishes, as well as lunch specials and delivery service in and near Calistoga. Open daily for lunch and dinner.

Specialty Stores & Markets

Cal Mart Grocery, 1491 Lincoln Ave., Calistoga, CA 94515; (707) 942-6271; www.calmartnv.com. Eventually you will see everyone you know in Calistoga at this market—it's the only full-service grocery in town. Proprietor Bill Shaw started working here in his teens as a bottle sorter and bagger. Ten years later he bought the store and has operated it ever since, for more than 30 years. Cal Mart has all the departments a good grocery store should have, along with a hot food bar, take-away rotisserie chickens, and many local artisanal products. So if you crave a box of Ritz crackers to pair with the rare Goat's Leap Sumi made in Napa Valley and sold in the cheese department, Cal Mart can hook you up. Ask for Patti McBride, Cal Mart's chatty "cheese lady," for more recommendations.

Calistoga Roastery, 1426 Lincoln Ave., Calistoga, CA 94515; (707) 942-5757; www.calistoga roastery.com; $. Good coffee isn't hard to find in Calistoga, but this shop has been roasting beans for two decades, and supplying their products to many inns, restaurants, and hotels in Napa Valley, too. So it's considered the granddaddy of the coffee purveyors in this town. Owner Clive Richardson has operated the Roastery in Calistoga since 1992, and it's been in its current location since 2004. Clive keeps busy with the wholesale and mail-order side of the business, along with selling the Roastery's coffee in such Napa Valley stores as Cal Mart, Vallerga's Market, and Sunshine Foods. The Roastery is roomy, with lots of tables. The freshly baked breakfast pastries, bagels, granola, sandwiches, salads, and fruit smoothies are reliable staples. Stake your claim on a stool at the window and watch Calistoga cruise by.

San Marco Cafe, 1408 Lincoln Ave., Calistoga, CA 94515; (707) 942-0714. The sign advertises coffee, but it's the sugary stuff that brings people in to this tiny store, barely large enough to turn around in. San Marco can brew an espresso or cappuccino, sure, but your sweet tooth will be drawn to the ice cream, shakes, smoothies, cookies, brownies, and other delights. If that's not enough stimulation, ask about their free advice.

Scoops & Swirls, 1473 Lincoln Ave., Calistoga, CA 94515; (707) 341-3132. When it's time for ice cream, Scoops & Swirls is among the best. The colorful assortment of flavors makes it difficult to choose. Four flavors of frozen yogurt are also dished out, as well as coffee and hot chocolate. Beware: the single scoops are big.

Vallarta Market, 1009 Foothill Blvd. (Hwy. 29), Calistoga, CA 94515; (707) 942-8864. Many of the Latin markets in Napa Valley also have a food-to-go counter, and I'm so grateful they do. Vallarta Market is known for its reasonably priced, large selection of freshly prepared take-away Mexican food, with burritos for about six bucks and tacos under two bucks. The usual assortment of meats is offered (*carnitas, pastor, pollo,* and *asada*) to more intriguing tastes such as *lengua* (beef tongue), *chicharron* (fried pork rind), *buche* (pork stomach), and *cabeza* (beef head). Grab a container of prepared mole sauce on your way out, for making your own Mexican cuisine at home. This market is not on the main street through the commercial center of town (Lincoln Avenue); it's south of the intersection with the flashing red stoplight and across the street from the **Wine Garage** (see below).

Village Bakery, 1353 Lincoln Ave., Calistoga, CA 94515; (707) 942-1443. In a small town, sometimes a bakery is more than just a bakery. Calling itself a European-style bakery, this one also serves  gelato (12 flavors), and sells products by other food purveyors, such as jars of honey from Lake County to the north and marmalades by Hurley Farms to the south. The baker's signature sourdough bread won a gold medal at the 2010 Sonoma County Harvest Fair (the bakery is based in Sonoma County, with two other locations there). Box lunches are also offered, as are cold and grilled sandwiches, soups, salads, and quiche. The chandeliers add a touch of elegance. Look for the statue of the roly-poly chef outside the entrance.

Wine Garage, 1020 Foothill Blvd. (Hwy. 29), Calistoga, CA 94515; (707) 942-5332 or (888) 690-WINE; www.wine garage.net. This nontraditional wine shop's credo is clear: no bottle costs more than $25. Owner Todd Miller stocks exceptional small-production boutique labels from throughout California, and many from Napa Valley. To build inventory at his shop in Calistoga, Todd hatched a bold plan: find great regional wines at the source, subject them to a personal taste test ("If I don't love it, I don't buy it," he says), and price them inexpensively. That approach has worked well for Todd ("no cellar left unturned" is his mantra), and loyal customers love the Wine Garage, which is named for the former gas station it inhabits. Wine Garage also sells its own private-label Rhône and Bordeaux blends in jugs, the equivalent of about two-and-a-half regular-size bottles.

Yo el Rey Roasting, 1217 Washington St., Calistoga, CA 94515; (707) 942-1180; www.yoelrey.com. A relative newcomer to Calistoga (since 2008), Yo el Rey claims to be the first and only solely fair-trade, organic, single-origin micro-roastery and retail coffee shop in Napa Valley. It's small, with eclectic art on the walls for sale, and has the feel of a coffee shop you might find in San Francisco's Haight district. The art exhibits rotate frequently—one month it might be photography, the next month watercolors. In the bookcase is a collection of reading material from the owner's personal library, which you are welcome to peruse as you enjoy the java. On the speakers is cool jazz or reggae.

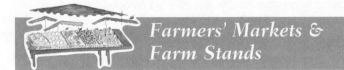

Farmers' Markets & Farm Stands

Calistoga Farmers' Market, Washington Street near the Police Department and Sharpsteen Museum, Calistoga, CA 94515; (707) 942-8892; www.calistogafarmersmarket.org. Fresh vegetables and fruits grown nearby are staples at this event, while local restaurants such as JoLé and Home Plate Cafe supply the breakfast and bakery goodies. Vendors pitching olive oils and vinegars, fresh seafood, smoked salmon, ornamental plants, prepackaged foods, intriguing arts and crafts, and fresh flowers can always be counted on to participate. Live music, too, ranging from bouncy acoustic rock to bluegrass and jazz. The market takes place on Saturday morning, May through Oct, from 8:30 a.m. to noon.

Calistoga Pottery, 1001 Foothill Blvd., Calistoga, CA 94515; (707) 942-0216; www.calistogapottery.com. If you admired the stoneware under your entrée at Bottega in Yountville or at Tra Vigne in St. Helena, or have spit into the lovely cuspidors in the tasting rooms at Robert Mondavi Winery or Beaulieu Vineyards, chances are they were made at this small husband-and-wife pottery factory. Jeff and Sally Manfredi have been firing clay here for more than 30 years, producing innovative dinnerware, serving pieces, and "spitters" for numerous businesses throughout Napa Valley. They do custom work for chefs and will do it for you, too. Walk up the short driveway into the showroom (the door to the left) to see the colorful assortment of stoneware for sale in all sizes. The manufacturing takes place in the adjoining room. All of the Manfredis' creations are lead-free and microwave and dishwasher safe, so they really are designed for everyday use, not for gathering dust on a shelf. When you visit (the pottery is open daily), Jeff will likely be in his apron, turning the wheel, while Sally applies glazes and finishing touches to the inventory. The two will gladly stop what they're working on to show you around, explain how to care for the stoneware, and offer suggestions for dining and sightseeing in Calistoga.

Forni Brown Welsh Gardens, 1214 Pine St. (at Cedar St.), Calistoga, CA 94515; (707) 942-6123. Look at your restaurant menu carefully—you're likely to see "Forni Brown Welsh" listed in the descriptions of the dishes featuring greens. Not far from downtown Calistoga, surrounded by mature residential neighborhoods, this 7-acre enterprise is growing the salad greens served at many of the great restaurants in Napa Valley, San Francisco, and around the nation. As a wholesaler to the trade, the business is not open to the public except in spring for an annual sale (see listing in Food Events & Happenings). Owners Peter Forni, Lynn Brown, and Barney Welsh were brought together serendipitously more than 30 years ago when "California cuisine" was the hot, new trend in restaurant kitchens everywhere. Their early customers included a San Francisco chef on the fast track to stardom and the gone-but-not-forgotten Rose et LeFavour gourmet restaurant in St. Helena. The threesome quickly gained a reputation for growing outstanding organic produce, and soon added the French Laundry in Yountville and Berkeley's Chez Panisse to their client list. Though many of the top restaurant chefs in the region now have their own small plots to grow herbs and greens, the name "Forni Brown Welsh Gardens" can still be found on many menus in Napa Valley and beyond.

Food & Wine Pairings/ Landmark Wineries

B Cellars, 400 Silverado Trail, Calistoga, CA 94515; (707) 709-8787; www.bcellars.com. The fountain made from an old wine press and the brilliant red umbrellas on the terrace alert you to the entrance to B Cellars. The winery set out to break winemaking custom, and make no apologies for it. Just south of Calistoga, B (for brix, the measurement of sugar content in wine grapes) offers a selection of appetizers in its tasting room that pair well with Blend 23, a brave mixture of Chardonnay, Sauvignon Blanc, and Viognier. (One taster said Blend 23 has notes of orange peel, lemon, and—wait for it—daffodils.) Not a fan of white wine? This one might change your mind. B's reds are more in line with Napa Valley tradition: Blend 24 is Tuscan style, made of Cabernet Sauvignon, Petite Sirah, and Sangiovese; Blend 25 is a combo of Cabernet Sauvignon and Syrah; and Blend 26 is a reserve Cabernet Sauvignon. B Cellars also produces Syrahs with grapes from the Carneros region and from hillside vineyards on Mt. Veeder, near the city of Napa. For $15 per person, walk-ins can taste four wines accompanied by an olive, cheese, and charcuterie plate. For $40 per person (and prior reservations) up to 20 people can experience a food-and-wine pairing conducted by a chef. These take place at 11 a.m. Wed through Sun. The winery is open daily from 10 a.m. to 5 p.m.

Castello di Amorosa, 4045 St. Helena Hwy. (Hwy. 29), Calistoga, CA 94515; (707) 967-6272; www.castellodiamorosa.com. This is a genuine 21st-century castle/winery, circa 2007, with moat and drawbridge, five towers, more than 100 rooms, a dungeon and torture chamber, and even a church that conducts Latin Mass on Sunday mornings. What does that have to do with food and wine?

For $68 per person, you can reserve a pairing event to taste Passito (a late harvest Semillon) with *foie gras;* a Chardonnay with triple-cream cheese; a Sangiovese with a mini slider of beef, lamb, and turkey; a Super-Tuscan blend with milk chocolate and French vanilla ganache; and a Gewürztraminer with sea-salt chocolate. That's a whole meal. The castle was erected by Dario Sattui, proprietor of **V. Sattui Winery** (see the St. Helena chapter), a man who believes in giving visitors a full-on experience, à la Disney. A standard wine tasting without reservations costs $17 per person, while a premium tour and tasting, including an in-depth look inside the castle's many hidey-holes, is $32 per person. A horse-drawn vineyard tour is optional ($68), on Saturdays only by reservation. You can't see the winery from Highway 29, but you can weave on up the driveway and look around outside for no charge. Open daily from 9:30 a.m. to 4:30 p.m.

Chateau Montelena, 1429 Tubbs Ln., Calistoga, CA 94515; (707) 942-5105; www.montelena.com. Have you seen the 2008 movie *Bottle Shock*? It's not a great film, it's not even a really good film, but most of it was shot at this winery, in downtown Calistoga, and parts of neighboring Sonoma County, so it's worth watching for the scenery alone. Based on the true story of Montelena's rapid rise to fame after winning the 1976 Judgment of Paris Tasting (and starring one of my personal favorites, Alan Rickman), the filmmakers took quite a few liberties to tell the tale. The real story is just as compelling. Jim Barrett acquired the winery in 1972, after the property had languished for decades. The 1973 Chardonnay bottled by Barrett and his winemaker at that time, Miljenko "Mike" Grgich, won a blind tasting in Paris overseen by French judges. The judges were dumbfounded to discover they had voted for a California wine over one of their own. *Quelle horreur!* Thanks to an enterprising reporter who witnessed the event, his article about the judging in *Time* magazine caused a minor sensation. Thousands of new visitors descended on Napa Valley to see where the wine had been made, and oenophiles around the world were desperate to acquire bottles of the '73. Twenty years later, to commemorate the news that shocked the wine world, the Smithsonian Institution's National Museum of American History created an exhibit devoted to the 1976 Paris tasting. A bottle of Montelena's 1973 Chardonnay is now part of the museum's permanent collection. Today, Montelena welcomes visitors to the tasting room to sample its food-friendly Chardonnay, or the Cabernet Sauvignon, Zinfandel, and Riesling. A "Bottle Shock and Chardonnay Experience" tour is offered for $25 per person on Thurs and Sun, with prior reservations. Without reservations, take a self-guided walk around the property and a jaunt to Jade Lake, with its crooked red footbridges, magnificent swans, and lovely views. Open 9:30 a.m. to 4 p.m. daily.

Clos Pegase, 1060 Dunaweal Ln., Calistoga, CA 94515; (707) 942-4981; www.clospegase.com. South of Calistoga just off Highway 29 are two showplace wineries, practically across from each other on Dunaweal Lane: **Sterling Vineyards** (see next listing) and Clos Pegase. Michael Graves, the architect who designed Clos Pegase, was chosen through a competition and commissioned by the owner, Jan Shrem, to build "a temple to wine and art." Completed in 1987, the winery is an arresting sight, made even more impressive by its sculpture garden of modern art. Clos Pegase bottles several varietals, including Cabernet Sauvignon, Chardonnay, Merlot, and Sauvignon Blanc. Open daily from 10:30 a.m. to 5 p.m.

Sterling Vineyards, 1111 Dunaweal Ln., Calistoga, CA 94515; (800) 726-6136; www.sterlingvineyards.com. Sterling's Greek-influenced structure is high off the valley floor, reached only by an aerial tram, which sweeps peacefully over the trees on its way to the tasting room at the top. Once there, visitors can move about the winery at their own pace. The basic $25 fee includes the tram ride, complimentary tastes of five wines, and a logo glass. Reserve wine and VIP tasting experiences are available for a few dollars more. Sterling produces many wines, with an emphasis on Cabernet Sauvignon, Merlot, and Chardonnay. Relax on the winery's expansive south terrace overlooking the Valley for as long as you wish before boarding the tram for the ride back down the hill. Open Mon through Fri from 10:30 a.m. to 5 p.m. (weekends 10 a.m. to 5 p.m.).

Von Strasser Winery, 1510 Diamond Mountain Rd., Calistoga, CA 94515; (707) 942-0930; www.vonstrasser.com. Chocolate or cheese? Von Strasser conducts a wine-and-chocolate indulgence ($30 per person), or a comprehensive wine-and-cheese pairing ($40). Both take

place in the winery's cave, so be prepared for a chilly 55 degrees F environment any time of year. The tastings feature five wines paired with chocolates or cheese, an in-depth education in the pairings, and tours of the grounds and the cave. Von Strasser bottles several wines, including Cabernet Sauvignon, a reserve blend, a port, and a rosé. The winery is open by appointment only, so call to reserve these special food-and-wine combos.

Brewpubs & Microbreweries

Calistoga Inn Restaurant & Brewery, 1250 Lincoln Ave., Calistoga, CA 94515; (707) 942-4101; www.calistogainn.com. Order the porter. That's my recommendation, backed up by many thirsty friends. On a hot day, the patio at this brewery/restaurant/inn, perched beside a narrow channel of the Napa River, is the place to be in Calistoga for a cold brew made on the premises. The inn part of the business has been rolling out the welcome mat for guests since 1882, and the interior of the building is quaintly historic, but with country chic accents. The brewery came to life more than a century later, in 1987—the first in Napa Valley since Prohibition to brew beer commercially. It produces four beers under the Napa Valley Brewing Company label: a wheat ale, a red ale, a pilsner, and a porter. The seasonal beers are usually German Kolsch, Blitzen IPA, Belgian pale ale, and Dugan oatmeal stout. All of the beer made here is served here, on tap and in hand-filled, 22-ounce bottles.

It's a small enterprise, with only 450 barrels produced annually. Awards? Yes, including bronze and gold medals at the Great American Beer Fest in Colorado and blue ribbons at the California State Fair. Want a brewery tour on weekdays? Just call ahead. On the dinner menu, the fare ranges from paella to prime rib ($$$), a step up from typical brewpub grub. A bar menu is offered midafternoon. Occasionally, the restaurant holds a brewer's dinner, a 6-course meal paired with different microbrews, for $50 per person. And there's more: the inn's original 18 guest rooms, among the most historic and least expensive lodgings in Napa Valley. The inn is open daily, even holidays, for lunch and dinner.

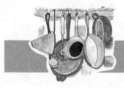

Learn to Cook

CasaLana, 1316 S. Oak St., Calistoga, CA 94515; (707) 942-0615 or (877) YOU-COOK; www.casalana.com, or www.gourmetretreats.com. Lana Richardson left the corporate world about 20 years ago to do something completely different, and CasaLana was born. After attending culinary school and starting her own catering company, Lana opened this 2-room bed-and-breakfast that specializes in gourmet cooking retreats. (Being a guest at the inn is not required, and Lana can help make arrangements for rooms elsewhere.) The class choices range from 5-hour afternoon sessions to 2-day retreats, 3-day retreats, and more. Topics are varied, and might focus on Latin flavors or summer grilling, knife selection and care, how to master the art of pie dough, the expert use of a pressure cooker, and so on. Menus are seasonal, incorporating herbs, vegetables, and fruits from the inn's gardens. At the end of each class, students dig in to enjoy the result of their labors. Prices are $175 per person for the 1-day classes and $650 for 3-day sessions (not including lodgings), and are usually limited to 8 students. Even more involved 5-day retreats are also offered. Lana's teaching kitchen is awash in natural light, with an awesome pantry and all the equipment needed to produce a gourmet meal. Lana can also arrange private parties and events, as well as corporate team-building cooking classes. See Chef Lana Richardson's recipe for **Semolina Flatbread with Caramelized Onions & Roasted Asparagus** on p. 222.

Craftsman Inn, 1213 Foothill Blvd., Calistoga, CA 94515; (707) 341-3035; www.thecraftsmaninn.com. There's a reason the guests at this classy 5-room bed-and-breakfast rave about the morning meal. The proprietors, Gillian and Nick Kite, know how to do it right. A professional chef, Gillian whips up exceptional granola, among other goodies, and all of the dishes served at breakfast are memorable. So if you're a guest at the inn, or even if you're staying elsewhere, Gillian can show you how to prepare a delicious lunch using seasonal, fresh ingredients. For $175 per person, the inn's well-equipped kitchen is turned into a classroom (10 students maximum) at midmorning.

Gillian selects an uncomplicated dish that students can make for themselves at home ("so they won't be scared to try it," she says). The 4-hour class concludes with students devouring their meal, along with Napa Valley wines. Included in the price is a night-before wine-and-food pairing where the participants can get to know each other. Classes are conducted midweek primarily from Dec to Mar, but the Kites can arrange customized sessions any time of year—give them a call to learn more. The inn is comfortable and stylish (consider booking the Spring room, my favorite), and is easy walking distance to the town's spas and other attractions.

Recipes

Chefs and culinary professionals are everywhere in Napa Valley, working at restaurants, wineries, bed-and-breakfasts, cooking schools, and catering businesses. They love the Valley for its abundant fresh ingredients and the opportunity to match their cuisine to the great wines produced in the region. This chapter features recipes created by a few of the Valley's many culinary artists, adapted for home cooks. You may not be as gifted in the kitchen as the French Laundry's Thomas Keller, but these recipes might inspire you to prepare a dish you wouldn't have considered otherwise.

Asparagus Soup with Mustard Greens & Cheddar/Mustard-Seed Crackers

In 2009, Chef Summer Sebastiani of All Seasons Bistro in Calistoga created this recipe at the last minute before entering it into the chef's competition at the Napa Valley Mustard Festival. Together with her kitchen staff, Summer whipped up this soup and raced off to the competition with only 5 minutes to spare before judging began. To her amazement, the soup won, and Summer was named Critic's Choice Chef of the Year for 2009.

Serves 6 to 8

- 2 tablespoons butter
- 2 large bunches of washed mustard greens (center stem cut away from the leaves and discarded), roughly chopped
- 1 shallot, peeled and sliced
- 2 quarts heavy cream
- 1 medium yellow onion, peeled and cut into slices
- 1 garlic clove, peeled

- 2 large bunches of asparagus, cut into 2-inch pieces
- 6 to 7 ounces baby spinach, thoroughly washed*
- 1 tablespoon fresh lemon juice
- Salt and pepper to taste
- Optional garnish: a sprinkle of mustard sprouts, available at natural food stores, or substitute radish sprouts

Melt butter in a large skillet and coat the bottom. Add the chopped mustard greens and sliced shallot. Gently sauté until the greens are completely soft and wilted. Taste the greens so you can ascertain how peppery and intense the flavors are, since you may decide not to use all that you've cooked. Set aside. Meanwhile, place cream, sliced onion, and the garlic clove in a heavy-bottomed 4-quart saucepan or a Dutch oven. Bring to a boil, drop temperature to a simmer, and cook until the onion and garlic are very soft, about 12 minutes (check for tenderness). Turn off burner, add asparagus, and let sit for 10 minutes or so to lightly cook the asparagus.

Add the cream and asparagus mixture to a blender and puree, alternating with the mustard greens and fresh spinach. Before adding the last of the mustard greens, taste the mixture to see if the flavor is pronounced. If you like the level of mustard flavor, don't add any more.

Pour the soup through a fine strainer, then add the lemon juice, and salt and pepper to taste.

Serve immediately, topped with a sprinkle of mustard sprouts and cheddar/mustard-seed crackers (see recipe), or cool to room temperature, cover, and refrigerate until use. Best served within two days.

* The delicate baby spinach doesn't really alter the soup's flavor, but the fresh, brilliant green color it provides is worth the addition.

Cheddar/Mustard-Seed Crackers

- 2 cups all-purpose flour
- 4 tablespoons cornmeal
- 2 teaspoons salt
- ½ teaspoon nutmeg, freshly grated if possible
- Small dash of cayenne pepper, approximately ⅛ teaspoon (or substitute a few grinds of black pepper)
- 2 ounces cold butter, cut into small pieces
- 1 cup good white cheddar cheese, such as Vermont, grated
- 1 cup finely grated Parmesan cheese
- ½ cup half-and-half
- 2 tablespoons whole mustard seeds

Briefly blend flour, cornmeal, salt, nutmeg, and cayenne together in a food processor, then sprinkle butter over the ingredients. Blend briefly, then continue pulsing just until combined and the mixture has a sandy-pebbly texture. Don't overmix.

Combine cheddar, Parmesan, half-and-half, and mustard seeds in a bowl, then slowly add this to the dough, just until nicely combined. The dough should be fairly firm and easy to form into a ball. Divide the dough and shape into two neat, even logs. Wrap tightly in plastic wrap and chill in refrigerator for at least three hours.

Preheat oven to 350 degrees. Slice the logs into thin rounds and place on a baking sheet lined with parchment paper. Bake for about 10 minutes, check for even browning, and rotate the pan if necessary. Bake for another 5 minutes. Let cool completely on the baking sheet, then place the crackers in an air-tight container. If not used within a few days, refresh the crackers in the oven at moderate temperature for 2 to 3 minutes to ensure crispness.

Courtesy of Chef Summer Sebastiani of All Seasons Bistro (p. 192).

Semolina Flatbread with Caramelized Onions & Roasted Asparagus

This recipe is just one example of the many creations of Chef Lana Richardson, who operates CasaLana bed-and-breakfast in Calistoga and conducts culinary classes (see the Learn to Cook category).

Serves 8

For the dough

1 teaspoon active dry yeast

½ cup warm water (105 degrees to 110 degrees)

½ teaspoon sugar

1 cup all-purpose flour

½ cup fine semolina flour

1 teaspoon kosher salt

2 teaspoons olive oil

Sprinkle the yeast in the water, and mix to dissolve. Add the sugar and mix. Let stand for a few minutes until it foams (known as proofing the yeast).

In a mixer with dough hook (can also be done in food processor with metal blade or by hand in a bowl), add the yeast/water mixture and ½ cup of the all-purpose flour. Process 1 to 2 minutes, scraping the bowl as needed, until the dough is mixed and elastic. Mix the remaining flour (all-purpose and semolina) and the salt. Add the flour and the oil to the dough, and process to mix until the dough forms a ball. If needed, add more water to help the dough come together.

Put the dough on a lightly floured surface and knead for a couple minutes until smooth. The dough will be fairly stiff. When the dough resists stretching and shrinks back quickly, it's ready. Put dough into a lightly oiled bowl, cover with a light towel, and set in a warm place to rise for one hour. Remove towel, punch down dough, and cover with towel again. Set in warm place for 15 minutes.

For the topping

2 tablespoons olive oil
2 tablespoons unsalted butter
2 yellow onions, sliced thin
1 bay leaf
2 tablespoons white wine
2 tablespoons fresh thyme
    leaves, chopped

½ teaspoon kosher salt
½ teaspoon fresh cracked black
    pepper
½ bunch asparagus, roasted
4 ounces chèvre

Combine the oil and butter in a heavy-bottomed sauté pan on medium-low heat. When hot, add the sliced onions and bay leaf and cook until onions are translucent and limp, about 5 to 8 minutes. Reduce the heat to low, cover, and cook for 15 to 20 minutes until onions are sweet and beginning to caramelize.

Remove the cover, turn heat to medium high, and add the wine. Continue to cook until the onions are fully caramelized. Add the thyme, season with salt and pepper, remove from heat, and set aside.

While the onions are caramelizing, prepare the asparagus. Heat a sheet pan in a hot oven (450 degrees). Wash the asparagus and break off the tough ends. Toss the asparagus with extra virgin olive oil, and season with salt and pepper. Place the asparagus on the hot sheet pan and roast for approximately 10 to 15 minutes, shaking the pan halfway through. Remove from oven. Cut the ends into slices, leaving the tips in about three-inch lengths.

To assemble:

Preheat oven to 400 degrees. Roll out dough to about ⅛-inch thickness in desired shape—round if using a round pizza pan or rectangular for a sheet pan. Place the dough on the lightly oiled pan and brush the edges of the dough with olive oil. Bake the dough for 8 to 10 minutes until it begins to set and is lightly browned. Then add the toppings of caramelized onions, asparagus, and cheese. Bake for another 4 to 5 minutes until the crust is golden and crisp.

Courtesy of Chef Lana Richardson of CasaLana (p. 214).

French Toast Soufflé

Ken and Susie Pope, innkeepers at Cedar Gables Inn on Napa's Coombs Street, emphasize the "breakfast" in bed-and-breakfast. Guests can always count on something delicious and unforgettable from Susie, and yet not too complicated to prepare for themselves at home. This recipe is a good example: a few common ingredients, simple instructions, and assemble-ahead convenience.

Serves 8

Bread cubes, cut into half-inch squares, with crusts trimmed (approximately one loaf of sourdough French bread)

½ cup butter at room temperature

8 ounces cream cheese

½ cup maple syrup

16 large eggs

2 cups half-and-half

1½ teaspoons vanilla

Cinnamon for dusting

The night before:

Thoroughly butter a 9-by-13 inch baking dish.

Fill baking dish half full with bread cubes.

In small bowl in microwave, soften the butter, cream cheese, and maple syrup gently, in increments of 10 seconds for a 1,000-watt oven, until mixture is soft and pourable. Blend with a wire whisk (it's OK if it's a little lumpy).

Spoon mixture over the bread cubes and distribute evenly, all the way to the edges of the dish.

In a separate bowl, beat the eggs, half-and-half, and the vanilla until thoroughly mixed. Pour the egg mixture over the bread, making sure that all bread cubes are moistened.

Dust with cinnamon and store overnight in the refrigerator.

In the morning:

Preheat oven to 375 degrees and bake for 30 minutes.

Lower the temperature to 350 degrees and bake for another 30 minutes. Watch carefully—the dish is done when the center is raised and firm and the top is slightly browned.

Cut into 8 servings. Top with diced strawberries, chopped pecans, and maple syrup, and dust with powdered sugar.

Courtesy of Susie Pope of Cedar Gables Inn (p. 101).

Rancho Gordo's Posole Verde

Created exclusively for this book, this stew is Steve Sando's variation on his tried-and-true posole verde, with posole as the basic ingredient. Also known as hominy, posole is dried corn that's been specially processed to be more digestible. Before adding it to this recipe, it must first be soaked and simmered (see note in recipe). Rancho Gordo sells posole online, along with cooking instructions, in case you can't find it where you live. Steve is also passionate about the heirloom beans he sells, like the Mayacoba used in this recipe, and he knows the best ways to bring out their full flavor.

Serves 4 to 6

½ cup plus 2 tablespoons extra-virgin olive oil

1 medium white onion, peeled and halved

4 garlic cloves, peeled

20 small tomatillos, husked and rinsed

1 fresh jalapeño pepper

2 poblano peppers

1 cup coarsely chopped cilantro

2 teaspoons dried Rancho Gordo Mexican Oregano

5 cups chicken broth (or vegetable broth)

2 cups cooked Rancho Gordo posole (note: dry posole should be soaked overnight in fresh water to cover, drained, then covered again with fresh water and simmered gently until tender, about three hours—many of the kernels will split open)

1 cup cooked Mayacoba beans (or cannellini beans)

Salt and freshly ground black pepper

2 limes, cut in wedges, for garnish

Put a large, dry skillet (preferably cast-iron or stainless steel) over a medium-high flame and let it get nice and hot, a good 2 minutes. Using ½ cup of the oil, lightly toss the onion, garlic, and tomatillos to coat. With a paper towel, rub the skin of the jalapeño with oil. Lay the vegetables in the hot pan and roast, turning occasionally, until soft and well charred on all sides, about 10 minutes.

Allow the vegetables to cool. Peel the skin from the jalapeño and remove the stem. Transfer the vegetables to a blender and purée in batches until completely smooth. Put the batches of purée into a large stockpot as you work.

Rub the poblanos with the remaining 2 tablespoons of oil and roast on a very hot grill, over a gas flame, or under a broiler, until the skins are blistered and blackened on all sides. Put the peppers in a bowl, cover with plastic wrap, and let sweat for about 10 minutes to loosen the skins. Peel and rub off the charred skins, pull out the cores, and remove the seeds. Put the poblanos, along with any collected juices, into the blender and purée until smooth; add to the stockpot.

Purée the cilantro, oregano, and broth together in the blender. Add this green purée to the stockpot also. Place the pot over medium heat, add the posole and beans, and season with salt and pepper to taste. Stir everything together and simmer, uncovered, for 20 minutes. Serve with lime wedges.

Courtesy of Steve Sando of Rancho Gordo New World Specialty Food (p. 64).

Seared Scallops with Warm Crab Beurre Blanc

Chris Aken of Avia Kitchen raised the bar for hotel restaurant cuisine when he came on board as executive chef at Avia Hotel in downtown Napa, which opened in 2009. The chef uses seasonal ingredients to keep the restaurant's menu fresh, and much of the produce used in the spring and summer dishes is grown nearby. This recipe is remarkably simple to prepare and looks elegant when plated. Make certain to use the freshest seafood you can find.

Serves 4

8 pieces of jumbo asparagus
8 pieces fresh sea scallops
1 teaspoon olive oil
Salt and pepper
2 tablespoons white wine

2 tablespoons lemon juice
1 tablespoon butter
1 pound fresh, cooked crab meat
1 bunch of chives (minced)

To Prepare the Asparagus

Clean asparagus and trim off the woody part of the stems. Blanch in boiling water until tender, 1 to 2 minutes, and then shock them in ice water. Be careful not to overcook or leave in the ice bath for too long, as they will absorb the water and become tasteless.

Once cooked and cooled, reserve the asparagus for later use.

To Prepare the Scallops

Source your seafood from a market or a monger that you trust. Pick large, dry scallops that are firm and smell of seawater. Before cooking, remove the muscle that attaches the scallop to the shell, then pat each scallop dry for best results.

Sear the scallops in a nonstick pan in olive oil. Do not crowd the scallops in the pan. Sear for about 2 minutes on each side, or to desired temperature.

Once cooked, remove the scallops from the pan, season with salt and pepper, then set in a warm place while you prepare the sauce.

To Prepare the Sauce

In the same pan that you cooked the scallops in, add the white wine and lemon juice. (Be careful, as wine can flame up if the pan is hot or if the wine is introduced to an open flame.) Cook the lemon juice and wine on low heat until it is reduced by half.

At this point add the butter and whisk carefully to create the butter sauce. Once the butter is emulsified with the lemon juice and wine, add the crab to the pan and remove from heat. You just want to warm the crab in the sauce (remember, the crab is already cooked).

Add the chives and fold gently into the sauce.

To Assemble

Lay the asparagus onto your favorite platter and artfully arrange the warm scallops. Cover the scallops and asparagus with the warm butter and crab sauce.

Courtesy of Chef Chris Aken of Avia Kitchen in the Avia Hotel (p. 36).

Crispy Fried Green Beans
with Hot Mustard Sauce

This recipe cries out for fresh-from-the-garden green beans. If you order this dish at Brix in Yountville, it's very likely the beans really were picked right outside in the extensive vegetable and herb gardens from which the restaurant sources many of its ingredients.

Serves 4 to 6

For the green beans

1 cup all purpose flour
2 tablespoons baking powder
1 teaspoon sugar
¼ teaspoon turmeric
1¼ cups water (ice cold)

2 pounds of green beans, washed and trimmed
6 cups canola oil
Kosher salt and black pepper (to taste)

Combine flour, baking powder, sugar, and turmeric. Whisk water into dry ingredients.

Lightly coat beans with batter and fry in 350-degree oil until crispy (about 2 minutes).

Remove beans from oil, season with salt and pepper, and place on paper towel to drain.

Place green beans on serving platter with small container of mustard sauce (recipe follows).

For the mustard sauce

¼ cup Coleman's dry mustard
½ cup rice wine vinegar
1 tablespoon yellow miso paste

⅓ cup agave nectar
2 egg yolks

Combine all ingredients in a mixing bowl and whisk until smooth.

Place bowl over a pot of simmering water and cook until thick, whisking frequently.

Courtesy of Brix (p. 113).

Lamb Kebabs with Cilantro Mint Pesto

In addition to bottling wine and olive oil and growing vegetables, Somerston Ranch raises lambs high in the hills overlooking Napa Valley. So they know a thing or two about preparing fresh leg of lamb in creative ways that pair well with their wines. This recipe is best served with Petite Sirah, preferably Somerston's Priest Ranch label.

Serves 6 to 8

For the pesto

1 cup fresh mint leaves

1 cup fresh cilantro leaves

2 tablespoons pine nuts

2 tablespoons grated Parmesan cheese

1 tablespoon fresh lemon juice

2 medium garlic cloves, peeled

½ teaspoon coarse kosher salt

½ cup Somerston olive oil

Salt and pepper to taste

For the kebabs

2 tablespoons olive oil

4 large garlic cloves, minced

2 teaspoons coarse salt

1 teaspoon ground coriander seeds

2 pounds trimmed boneless leg of lamb, cut into 1½-inch cubes

2 large red peppers, cut into 1-inch squares

1 large sweet onion, cut into 1-inch squares

6 to 8 metal skewers

Pepper, to taste

To Prepare the Pesto

Blend the first seven ingredients in a food processor to coarse puree.

With machine running, gradually pour in ½ cup olive oil, and puree until almost smooth.

Transfer pesto to a bowl and season with salt and pepper.

To Prepare the Kebabs

Mix 1 tablespoon oil, the garlic, coarse salt, and coriander in a medium bowl. Add lamb cubes and toss to coat. Cover and chill at least 2 hours and up to 4 hours.

Prepare grill to medium-high heat. Thread lamb cubes on skewers, alternating with peppers and onions. Place on a baking sheet, brush with oil, and sprinkle with pepper.

Grill to desired doneness, turning occasionally, 7 to 9 minutes for medium-rare.

Arrange kebabs on a platter and drizzle each with the pesto.

Courtesy of Somerston Ranch (p. 124).

Angel Hair with Clams, Chorizo, Saffron, Orange, Tomato & Cilantro

Matched with the food-friendly, bright acid note of the Benessere Vineyards 2007 Sangiovese, this pasta dish echoes its Mediterranean heritage. It was developed for Benessere by Eric G. Hensel, a Court of Master Sommeliers Certified Sommelier, and it's simple to prepare.

Serves 4

- 3 tablespoons extra-virgin olive oil
- 8 ounces bulk chorizo, or links with casings removed
- 2 large garlic gloves, peeled and thinly sliced
- 1 pound clams, preferably Manila, well scrubbed
- 1 cup low-sodium chicken broth
- ¼ cup fresh orange juice
- 1 medium bay leaf
- 1 large pinch of saffron threads
- Sea salt and fresh ground black pepper
- 1 pound angel hair pasta
- 3 oranges, peeled and divided into segments
- 1 large beefsteak tomato or 4 plum tomatoes, peeled and seeded, and chopped
- 2 tablespoons whole cilantro leaves

Bring a large pot of lightly salted water to a boil.

Heat the olive oil in a large sauté pan over medium-high heat. Add the chorizo and garlic and cook, breaking up the chorizo with a wooden spoon, until browned, 5 to 6 minutes.

Add the clams, chicken broth, orange juice, bay leaf, and saffron. Cover and cook until the clams open, about 7 to 8 minutes. Season to taste with salt and pepper.

Add the pasta to the boiling water and cook until al dente, about 2 minutes less than what the package advises. Drain the pasta and return to the pot.

Pour the clam mixture into the pot, place over low heat, and toss the pasta with the sauce for 1 minute to allow it to marry and absorb. Add the orange segments and chopped tomato, toss, and cook for another minute. The pasta should still be firm to the bite.

Transfer the complete dish to a warm platter. Remove and discard the bay leaf and any unopened clams. Sprinkle with the cilantro and serve immediately.

Courtesy of Benessere Vineyards (p. 175).

Orzo & Green Bean Salad with Cucumbers, Apples & Parsley Vinaigrette

Sandy Dominguez, a demonstration chef at the Culinary Institute of America at Greystone (CIA), created this refreshing side-dish salad loaded with healthful ingredients. When you attend one of the CIA's weekend cooking demonstrations, Sandy is likely to be the chef presiding over the range. She also teaches many of the CIA's food enthusiast classes.

Serves 6 as a side dish

For the salad

8 ounces green beans, trimmed

8 ounces whole-wheat orzo (1¼ cups)

2 cups diced cucumbers (about 8 ounces)

¾ cup diced apples

1 avocado, peeled and diced

Salt and pepper to taste

¼ cup sliced almonds, toasted

½ cup high-quality aged goat cheese, crumbled

For the dressing

⅔ cup (packed) chopped fresh parsley

2 tablespoons white balsamic vinegar

1 tablespoon fresh lemon juice

1 teaspoon grated lemon zest

¼ teaspoon crushed red chile flakes

¼ cup olive oil

1 teaspoon salt

Fresh ground black pepper to taste

Cook green beans in large saucepan of boiling salted water until just tender, about 5 minutes. Using a slotted spoon, transfer the beans to a bowl of ice water to "shock" or stop them from cooking further; set aside. Add orzo to the same boiling water. Cook until tender, stirring occasionally.

Meanwhile, blend the parsley, vinegar, lemon juice, lemon zest, and chile flakes in a blender or mini food processor, slowly drizzling in the olive oil until almost smooth. Season the dressing with salt and pepper.

Drain the orzo and toss with some of the dressing until well coated so it won't stick together, and cool.

Cut beans crosswise into ½-inch pieces. Place in a large bowl. Add the orzo, cucumber, apples, and avocado; mix in remainder of dressing. Season with salt and pepper to taste.

Top with sliced almonds and the crumbled goat cheese.

Courtesy of Chef Sandy Dominguez of the Culinary Institute of America at Greystone (p. 189).

Apricot Tart with Cornmeal Crust

Claiming to be the oldest catering company in Napa Valley (since 1975), Knickerbockers' (1314 Oak Ave., St. Helena, CA 94574; 707-963-9278; www .knickerbockerscatering.com) has a reputation for excellence and innovation. Their apricot tart recipe has received wide acclaim, with the cornmeal adding extra texture and flavor to the crust. This tart can be served with or without the sweet apricot sauce—also great on ice cream or pound cake—and whipped cream.

Serves 8

For the crust

1½ cups all-purpose flour
¾ cup cornmeal
¾ teaspoon salt
¾ cup (1½ sticks) unsalted
    butter, at room temperature

¾ cup sugar
3 large egg yolks

For the apricot filling

5 cups water
12 ounces dried apricot halves
    (about 2⅔ cups)
1 teaspoon vanilla extract

⅓ cup apricot preserves
1 large egg, beaten to blend
3 tablespoons sugar

For the apricot sauce

2 cups (or more) water
⅔ cup sugar

⅔ cup dried apricot halves
    (about 3 ounces)
1 teaspoon vanilla extract

To Prepare the Crust

Whisk the flour, cornmeal, and salt in a small bowl to blend. Using an electric mixer, beat the butter and sugar in a large bowl to blend. Beat in egg yolks. Add the dry ingredients and beat just until blended.

Divide the dough in half and flatten into disks. Wrap each dough disk in plastic and refrigerate for 20 minutes. (Dough can be prepared a day ahead; keep it refrigerated and let it soften slightly at room temperature before using.)

To Prepare the Filling

Bring 5 cups water to a simmer in a heavy medium pot over medium heat. Add the apricots and poach until tender, about 25 minutes. Drain well, then mix the vanilla extract gently into the apricots.

To Assemble the Tart

Preheat oven to 375 degrees. Lightly oil a 9-inch diameter tart pan with removable bottom.

Unwrap 1 dough disk and press onto the bottom and up the sides of tart pan. Spread apricot preserves over the bottom of the crust. Place poached apricots over the preserves, covering the crust completely and overlapping slightly. Using a pastry brush, brush the beaten egg over edges of crust.

Roll out the second dough disk between two sheets of parchment paper to a 12-inch round. Remove the top piece of paper. Using a 1-inch diameter cookie cutter, cut a hole in center of top crust. Turn crust over filled tart pan. Remove the second piece of paper and press crust around edges to seal. Cut off excess dough to make the top crust flush with the tart pan sides. Brush crust with beaten egg and sprinkle with 3 tablespoons sugar.

Bake the tart until the cornmeal crust is golden brown, about 45 minutes. Transfer to a rack to cool for 30 minutes. Remove the tart from pan and cool completely. Serve with apricot sauce and whipped cream, if desired.

To Prepare the Apricot Sauce

Combine 2 cups water, sugar, and dried apricots in a heavy medium sauce pan. Bring the mixture to a boil. Reduce heat to medium and simmer until the apricots are tender, about 25 minutes. Remove from heat and cool for 15 minutes.

Transfer the apricot mixture to a blender and puree, adding more water by the tablespoon if needed to form a smooth sauce. Add the vanilla extract and blend well. Makes about 1½ cups.

Courtesy of Knickerbockers' Oak Avenue Catering.

Meyer Lemon & Ancho Chile Chicken

Developed by Round Pond winery chef Hannah Bauman, this recipe uses brightly flavored Meyer lemon olive oil to bring out the best in grilled chicken paired with lightly grilled ripe avocados. It's easy to prepare and looks great on the serving platter.

Serves 5 to 7

3 to 4 pounds of chicken pieces (such as breasts with ribs attached, or the leg/thigh combo)

Round Pond Meyer Lemon olive oil to drizzle

4 whole ripe avocados, halved and with pits removed

3 whole lemons, halved·

Salt and pepper

For the marinade

3 cloves garlic

2 tablespoons fresh thyme leaves, picked from the stems

Grated zest of 2 lemons

1 dried ancho chile (or 1 teaspoon ancho chile powder)

1 to 2 tablespoons kosher salt

1 to 2 teaspoons fresh cracked black pepper

½ cup Round Pond Meyer Lemon olive oil

½ cup chicken stock

1 tablespoon honey

Juice of 2 lemons

To Prepare the Marinade

Smash the garlic cloves, thyme, lemon zest, dried ancho chile or powder, salt, and pepper into a fine paste with a mortar and pestle or in a small blender or food processor. While blending, add 1 tablespoon Meyer lemon olive oil. Continue to pulverize the paste until blended smoothly with the oil.

Remove the paste and place in a large zip-lock bag. Add the remaining olive oil, chicken stock, honey, and lemon juice. Seal the bag and mix thoroughly with your hands to fully incorporate. Add the chicken to the bag, remove air from the bag, and seal tightly. Refrigerate for 2 to 4 hours, turning the bag twice.

To Grill

Prepare a hot charcoal fire on one side of a grill (or use low heat on a gas grill). Spread ¼ of the coals to the other side of the grill. Clean and season the grate when the coals are ready.

Place the chicken on the cooler side of the grill, skin side up. Cook for 15 to 20 minutes until the underside of the chicken is golden brown; brush with marinade. Flip chicken over, brush with marinade, and cook until juices run clear, about 10 to 15 minutes. Skin should be golden brown and chicken cooked through. Remove and let rest for 5 to 7 minutes.

During the last 10 minutes of grilling the chicken, drizzle the avocado halves with the Meyer lemon olive oil and sprinkle with salt and pepper. Place the halved avocados and the halved lemons on the grill, cut side down, and grill for 6 to 9 minutes. Flip over and grill for another 3 to 4 minutes.

Serve chicken with sliced, grilled avocados and a squeeze of the grilled lemons.

Courtesy of Chef Hannah Bauman of Round Pond Estate (p. 139).

Appendix A: Index of Foodie Faves & Landmark Eateries

Appendix B: Index of Purveyors

Index